Formative Assessment Strategies FOR Enhanced Learning IN Science, K–8

Formative Assessment Strategies FOR Enhanced Learning IN Science, K–8

Elizabeth Hammerman

CORWIN PRESS
A SAGE Company

Copyright © 2009 by Corwin Press

For information:

Corwin Press
A SAGE Company
2455 Teller Road
Thousand Oaks, California 91320
www.corwinpress.com

SAGE Ltd.
1 Oliver's Yard
55 City Road
London, EC1Y 1SP
United Kingdom

SAGE India Pvt. Ltd.
B 1/I 1 Mohan Cooperative
  Industrial Area
Mathura Road, New Delhi 110 044
India

SAGE Asia-Pacific Pte. Ltd.
33 Pekin Street #02-01
Far East Square
Singapore 048763

Printed in the United States of America.

Library of Congress Cataloging-in-Publication Data

Hammerman, Elizabeth L.
Formative assessment strategies for enhanced learning in science, K-8/ Elizabeth Hammerman.
    p. cm.
Includes bibliographical references and index.
ISBN 978-1-4129-6296-4 (cloth) – ISBN 978-1-4129-6297-1 (pbk.)
1. Science--Study and teaching (Elementary)–United States–Evaluation
2. Educational tests and measurements–United States. I. Title.

LB1585.H28 2009
372.35'044–dc22

2008031919
This book is printed on acid-free paper.

08 09 10 11 10 9 8 7 6 5 4 3 2 1

Acquisitions Editor: Hudson Perigo
Editorial Assistant: Lesley K. Blake
Production Editor: Appingo Publishing Services
Cover Designer: Rose Storey

Contents

Preface

Research-based strategies for improving student learning through formative assessment have been the subject of many books and articles. This book synthesizes and highlights important messages and strategies offered by researchers, authors, and practitioners. What is unique here is that the tools and strategies for using formative assessment effectively are operationally defined and shown in the context of K–8 science.

Formative Assessment Strategies for Enhanced Learning in Science is a practitioner's guide that introduces teachers to formative assessment as a way of thinking and acting. The tools and strategies of formative assessment that are described in the chapters are those that classroom teachers can use to capture evidence of student thinking and learning in all disciplines. Numerous models and templates are provided to assist the practitioner in applying the strategies for high-quality teaching and formative assessment to their classroom practice.

THE GOALS OF *FORMATIVE ASSESSMENT STRATEGIES FOR ENHANCED LEARNING IN SCIENCE* ■

The purpose of this book is to describe and model tools and strategies for learning and assessment in the context of primary, intermediate, and middle grade science and to show how they support a formative assessment system and enhance learning.

The models shown are aligned with important learning goals related to the content, processes, and habits of mind that define the scientifically literate citizen. Carefully constructed formative assessments provide valuable information about student thinking and learning that can be used to monitor progress and inform and guide instruction. Formative assessments provide feedback to students, giving them a way to assume more responsibility for what they learn and how they learn.

Occasionally, readers of this book will be invited to complete exercises that require thought and reflection. The purpose of these exercises is to provide greater clarity about one's perspective and personal or schoolwide practices related to assessment while identifying areas that may need modification or change. The book offers an overview of practical ideas and strategies for formative assessment to guide the practitioner in planning effective instruction.

■ USES FOR *FORMATIVE ASSESSMENT STRATEGIES FOR ENHANCED LEARNING IN SCIENCE*

Formative Assessment Strategies for Enhanced Learning in Science is an excellent resource for science methods courses and teacher enhancement programs since it guides preservice and inservice teachers through a step-by-step approach to understanding how different tools of formative assessment can be used to enhance student learning. A research-based rationale for formative assessment is provided along with tools and strategies that are operationally defined and modeled in the context of science.

As a resource for professional development, *Formative Assessment Strategies for Enhanced Learning in Science* offers a study of the rationale and strategies for using formative assessment and rubrics to provide feedback and motivate students to higher levels of productivity. Through formative assessment, students become more aware of learning goals and expectations, use rubrics to guide their learning and to self-assess, and take responsibility for their learning.

Teachers will discover clear explanations and models that can be used to guide them in developing formative assessments and rubrics that align with their science curriculum. Workshops that engage teachers in the theory and practice of using formative assessments are worthwhile and beneficial to both teachers and students. Teachers focus on important goals and standards, implement more effective teaching methods, and use assessments to gauge student learning, inform instruction, and achieve goals. Students become more responsible and successful learners.

Acknowledgments

The work of many researchers and practitioners who helped to shape my understanding of assessment over the years is reflected in this book, and I am grateful for their contributions. I am truly indebted to Dr. Diann Musial, for the wit and wisdom she generously shared throughout our quest to create models of effective practice, and to Dr. Robert Yager, for his insightful questions and suggestions that helped guide this book and others in the series.

I wish to thank my editor, Hudson Perigo, and the amazing and talented staff of Corwin Press for their continued support throughout the writing and publishing process and beyond. And finally, I also want to give a special thank you to the reviewers whose feedback was both helpful and appreciated!

—Elizabeth Hammerman

PUBLISHER'S ACKNOWLEDGMENTS ■

Corwin Press would like to acknowledge the contributions of the following reviewers:

Elizabeth Alvarez
Area 10 Math and Science Coach
Chicago Public Schools
Chicago, IL

Regina Brinker, MS
Science Teacher
Christensen Middle School
Livermore, CA

John E. Bormann
Lead Teacher/Science Teacher
HW Mountz School
Spring Lake, NJ

Rose-Marie Botting
Retired, Science Curriculum Specialist
Broward County Schools, Florida
President, RMB Consultants, Inc.
Coral Springs, FL

Sandra K. Enger, PhD
Associate Professor of Science Education
The University of Alabama in Huntsville
Huntsville, AL

Judith A. Filkins
K–8 Math and Science
    Curriculum Coordinator
Lebanon School District
Lebanon, NH

Jenny Sue Flannagan, EdD
Director, Martinson Center for
    Mathematics and Science
Regent University
Virginia Beach, VA

Linda Keteyian
Teacher
Detroit Public Schools
Detroit, MI

Inez Fugate Liftig
Grade 8 Science Teacher
Fairfield Woods Middle School
Fairfield, CT

Dr. Gail H. Marshall, EdD
Assistant Professor
Department of Curriculum and Instruction,
    University of West Georgia
Carrollton, GA

Dr. Felicia M. Moore
Assistant Professor of Science Education
Teachers College, Columbia University
New York, NY

Senta A. Raizen
Director
National Center for Improving
    Science Education/WestEd
Washington, DC

Robert E. Yager
Professor
Science Education Center
University of Iowa
Iowa City, IA

About the Author

Elizabeth Hammerman is a dedicated Science Educator. Her background includes teaching science at the middle school and high school levels, instructing elementary and secondary science methods courses at the university level, and working extensively with K–12 science teachers in the field. She has served as a consultant, workshop facilitator, project director, instructional designer, and professional development provider for school districts, regional centers, state offices of education, and professional organizations.

Elizabeth is the author of numerous articles, instructional materials, and books. Recent publications—*Eight Essentials of Inquiry-Based Science* (2006), *Becoming a Better Science Teacher: Eight Steps to High Quality Instruction and Student Achievement* (2006), and *Differentiated Instructional Strategies in Science* (2008)—provide a vision for high-quality, standards-based science and offer practical, research-based tools and strategies for effective teaching and learning

Her Science Achievement professional development programs for teacher leaders and classroom teachers are designed to build leadership capacity and strengthen expertise needed to achieve excellence in teaching and learning in K–12 science.

Introduction

Clearly relating assessment tasks and products of student work to the valued goals of science education is integral to assessment plans.
—National Research Council [NRC], 1996, p. 91

New models of teaching and learning have evolved from brain research and the wisdom of professionals in the field that cause us to question our beliefs and assumptions about what is worth knowing and how students learn. Educational goals are linked to instruction and assessments in more authentic ways in standards-based classrooms than they are in text-driven classrooms. Instructional strategies are more accurately viewed as the means to the end rather than as an end in themselves, and assessments are regarded as diagnostic tools for monitoring student progress and guiding instruction toward successful learning.

STUDENT-CENTERED ■
INSTRUCTION AND ASSESSMENT

Although teachers have always been held accountable for what students learn in the classroom, science teaching and assessment often take the form of reading from textbooks and recalling information on forced choice tests. Even when laboratory investigations requiring higher-order thinking and problem solving are included in the instructional plan, the measures of student learning are often limited to recalling factual information, restating a definition, or applying a mathematical formula.

The National Science Education Standards endorsed an inquiry-based approach to instruction through which teachers select teaching and assessment strategies that guide and facilitate learning of important concepts and skills, orchestrate discourse about scientific ideas, respond to diversity, and use multiple methods to gather data about students' understanding and abilities (NRC, 1996).

> . . . the measures of student learning are often limited to recalling factual information . . .

The shift from teacher-centered to student-centered instruction and assessment puts more emphasis on developing understanding and responding to student needs and interests. Changing the teacher's role from one of provider of information to one of facilitator of learning requires them to have a strong commitment to teaching and learning that includes

- an understanding of the nature and content of the disciplines
- knowledge of and ability to implement skills and strategies for effective instruction
- an understanding of and respect for formative assessment as a powerful tool for promoting, enhancing, recognizing, and celebrating achievement (Black and Wiliam, 1998)

■ CHANGING PRACTICE TO IMPROVE LEARNING

Effective teaching mirrors effective learning. Thus, when students aren't learning, it is time to question the beliefs and policies that guide goal setting and the teaching and assessment practices that reflect them in the classroom. There is now a strong research base to support new approaches to classroom practice that promote higher standards and increase student achievement.

The journey toward more effective instruction and assessment is both bitter and sweet. On one hand, it requires administrators and teachers to invest time, effort, and resources in an ongoing process of professional development and change, but on the other hand, the rewards are great in terms of providing accountability for what students know and are able to do, as well as in increasing student motivation and achievement.

■ AN OVERVIEW OF CHAPTERS

The chapters that follow provide a research base and rationale for formative assessment and identify and operationally define strategies for embedding formative assessment into the science curriculum.

Chapter 1 operationally defines formative assessment and provides a way to reflect on current beliefs and practices related to assessment. A research-based rationale is provided for use in developing a vision for formative assessment to guide successful standards-based teaching and learning in standards-based science and technology education for the twenty-first century.

In Chapter 2, rubrics are described and shown as ways to identify the important indicators of learning for the development of scientific literacy and to communicate student strengths and weaknesses in reaching learning goals. Rubrics are powerful tools for enabling students to self-assess and take responsibility for learning.

Chapters 3–6 focus on the tools and strategies for enhancing instruction and gathering information about student learning from which to make informed decisions. Descriptions and standards-related models are provided in the context of K–8 science.

Chapter 7 provides a framework for planning and implementing high-quality instruction and formative assessment. The chapter includes a review of assessment strategies, planning guides with examples, and suggestions for differentiating instruction.

Figure 0.1 provides an overview of the chapters for reference.

Figure 0.1 Formative Assessment Strategies for Enhanced Learning in Science			
Chapter 1 Formative Assessment and Science	Chapter 2 Using Rubrics to Guide Learning	Chapter 3 Observation Checklists and Effective Questioning	Chapter 4 Notebooks, Reports, Graphic Organizers
• New Ways of Thinking About Assessment • Goal-Centered Assessment • Research Support for Formative Assessment • Creating a Vision for Formative Assessment • Examining Beliefs and Practices • Traditional Versus Student-Centered Views of Assessment • Formative Assessment as "Authentic" Assessment • Clear Targets for Instruction and Assessment	• The What and Why of Rubrics • Holistic Rubrics • Holistic Rubric for a Science Report • Limitations to Holistic Scoring • Designing Holistic Rubrics • Generalized Rubrics • Examples of Generalized Rubrics • Analytic Rubrics • Assessment Tasks With Analytic Rubrics • Designing Analytic Rubrics • Rubrics for Self-Assessment and Peer Assessment • Design a Rubric	• Observation Checklists • Sample Observation Checklists • Effective Questioning • Questions for Thinking and Problem Solving • Questions for Instruction and Assessment	• Notebooks • Notebooks as Assessment Tools • Rubric for a Science Notebook • Lab Reports • Lab Reports for Learning and Assessment • Rubric for a Lab Report • Graphic Organizers • Descriptive Organizers • Sequential Organizers • Process-Causal Organizers • Categorical Organizers • Comparison-Relational Organizers • Problem-Solution Organizers

(Continued)

Figure 0.1 (Continued)		
Chapter 5 Projects and Presentations	Chapter 6 Performance Tasks and Embedded Assessments	Chapter 7 Planning and Implementing Formative Assessment
• Learning Through Projects • Assessing Projects • Rubric for a Project • Learning Through Presentations • Assessing Presentations	• Performance Assessment • Performance Tasks • A Generalized Rubric for a Performance Task • Embedded Assessments • A Model for Embedded Assessment • Sample Embedded Performance Task • Designing Embedded Performance Assessments • Performance Assessments Following Instruction• Sample Performance Assessments • Performance Assessment as Benchmark Assessment • Characteristics of Benchmark Assessments • Sample Benchmark Assessment	• Characteristics of High-Quality Instruction and Assessment • Planning Formative Assessment • A Planning Guide for Formative Assessment • A Planning Guide for a Unit on Cells • Using Assessment Data to Modify Instruction • Project Choices • Adjusting Assignments • Stations for Active Learning• DifferentiatingInstruction Through Centers • Creating Contracts • Formative Assessment and Accountability

Formative Assessment and Science

When teachers are given the statement "When I think of assessment, I think of ..." they almost always complete the statement with the word "testing." This view of assessment results, in part, from beliefs and practices that stem from text-driven curricula where students study content in a chapter and then are given publisher-provided assessments in the form of multiple-choice, matching, or true/false items related to the content in the chapter. Questions often require students to select a response that was memorized or match terms to definitions. These classroom assessments are used to determine student learning and reward them for learning specific information within a specified time and in a particular way.

Views of classroom assessment are also influenced by the practice of using standardized tests to measure and communicate learning. Levels of performance on summative assessments are communicated through scores or grades that are often more important to students than the knowledge or skills they learned.

NEW WAYS OF THINKING ABOUT ASSESSMENT

In recent years the leaders in the assessment field have made serious attempts to explain the significant differences between assessments *of* learning and assessments *for* learning (Black, Harrison, Lee, Marshall, & Wiliam, 2004; Black & Wiliam, 1998; Marzano, 2000; Marzano & Kendall,

2007; Stiggins, 2002; Stiggins & Chappuis, 2006). Understanding this distinction requires a shift from thinking about assessment as a way of determining what students have learned following instruction or as a capstone performance to determine a score or grade to thinking about assessment as part of instruction intended to capture evidence of student learning for purposes of monitoring progress and guiding and improving instruction.

A first step in changing perceptions of assessment requires taking a critical look at assessment as a practice that has, essentially, three different purposes:

1. *Preassessments:* Preassessments are administered to students at the beginning of an instructional unit to identify prior knowledge or misconceptions they may have about a topic. Such information determines a reasonable starting point for instruction.

2. *Formative assessments*: Formative assessments are used throughout instruction to collect evidence of learning for purposes of monitoring progress and guiding instruction.

3. *Summative assessments:* Summative assessments generally take the form of paper-and-pencil tests, capstone performances, or a combination of the two, which follow instruction and are used to:

   - determine how well students "measure up" to a standard
   - compare students to one another and designate positions
   - assign grades

Assessments *for* learning serve a very different purpose than preassessments or summative assessments since their purpose is to provide meaningful feedback to teachers and students about student progress in reaching important learning goals. Scores on assessments for learning are used to inform, not to factor into a grade.

The information provided through formative assessments is used to monitor progress and direct students toward continued learning, relearning, or alternative learning to improve motivation and self-esteem. Reaping the rewards of formative assessment requires not only a shift in practice, but a different way of thinking about effective teaching and learning altogether.

◼ GOAL-CENTERED ASSESSMENT

Formative assessment is goal centered; that is, it focuses attention on successful teaching and learning of important learning goals and standards. This approach involves students in the teaching/learning process and offers opportunities for them to take responsibility for learning by setting personal goals and selecting strategies for meaningful learning. Through formative assessment, students compete with themselves rather than with other students.

A comprehensive view of classroom assessment is offered by Stiggins (1994). His principled view of classroom assessment points to the need for classroom teachers to be able to define and assess five kinds of learning goals—knowledge, reasoning, skills, product, and affective goals. This view of assessment aligns well with the broad range of goals and standards for science education, as well as other areas of the curriculum.

The goal-centered view of assessment challenges teachers to use assessments throughout learning to:

- monitor student progress in conceptual understanding and knowledge and use of skills
- capture evidence of thinking, reasoning, and problem-solving ability
- apply concepts and skills to technology and society through projects, products, and inventions
- provide information about the student's ability to work with others, communicate his or her ideas and understandings, show respect for living things, and demonstrate other dispositions.

Formative assessments capture evidence of student thinking and learning related to important concepts, skills, and habits of mind. Data and information gathered through formative assessments also inform curricular change and professional development needs. A comprehensive definition of formative assessment is offered in Figure 1.1.

RESEARCH SUPPORT FOR FORMATIVE ASSESSMENT

Educational research sends powerful messages to practitioners about what works to enhance student achievement. In their landmark study, Black and Wiliam (1998) surveyed over 580 articles and chapters in an effort to determine if improving formative assessment raises standards. The researchers found overwhelming evidence to support the fact that formative assessment is one of the most powerful tools for promoting effective learning. They also discovered that "improved formative assessment helps low achievers more than other students and so reduces the range of achievement while raising achievement overall" (p. 141).

Black and Wiliam (1998) also showed that achievement gains are greater when teachers involve students in the assessment process. They contend that students need to be trained in self-assessment in order to have a greater understanding of important learning goals and understand what they need to do to achieve success (p. 144). Thus, an essential component of formative assessment is student self-assessment.

Kohn (1999) described self-assessment as teachers and students working together to determine the criteria by which their learning will be assessed and having them do as much of the actual assessment as is practical. He contended that the process is less punitive, gives students control over their education, and provides enormous intellectual benefits (p. 209).

Kohn also cited studies that showed positive results when students were given choices, were involved in decision-making, and felt personally responsible for their learning. Studies reported that students completed more tasks in less time, improved self-esteem and perceived academic competence, and developed higher-level reading skills (pp. 222–223).

Figure 1.1 A Comprehensive View of Formative Assessment

Formative assessment is the practice of using a variety of tools and strategies as part of the instructional process to gather evidence of student thinking and learning from which to make informed decisions about each of these important educational issues.

- Instruction—what we teach, what we do, and how we do it
- Student learning—where they need to go and how to help them get there
- Differentiating instruction—build on student strengths and interests, correct their weaknesses, and provide for students who aren't learning
- Curricular enhancement, modification, and change—concepts to address more thoroughly and experiences to build into the curriculum
- Raising standards of student achievement

As well as . . .

- Professional development needs related to

> Content knowledge
> Pedagogy—teaching skills and effective practices
> Use of technology, resources, and equipment
> Learning communities
> Mentoring and coaching

In his study, *How Teaching Matters*, Wenglinsky (2000) linked classroom practices to academic performance in math and science using data from questionnaires to parents, teachers, and over seven thousand eighth-grade students who took the 1996 National Assessment of Educational Progress. Besides identifying characteristics of effective teachers, the study pointed to effective practices, one of which was implementing teacher-developed assessments into their lessons to provide frequent feedback to students about their learning.

Other studies focused on identifying policies and practices that define high-quality teaching and promote learning (Anderson & Stewart, 1997; Black et al., 2004; Ermeling, 2005; Stronge, 2002; Weiss, Pasley, Smith, Banilower, & Heck, 2003). These studies reported that effective teachers encourage interactions among students and between students and teachers and use assessment as a learning tool to provide frequent, constructive feedback to students and to monitor student progress.

Reeves (2008) contended that when grading practices improve, discipline and morale improve as well. He found remarkable changes in one challenging urban high school through focused attention on improved feedback and intervention for students. Positive changes included reduction in course failures, increase in enrollments in advanced placement courses, decline in sus-pensions, and a noticeable improvement in teacher morale and school climate.

The instructional power of formative assessment is echoed in the well-known meta-analysis of effective instructional strategies led by Marzano, Pickering, and Pollock (2001), which identified *providing feedback*—a central principle of formative assessment—as one of nine categories of instructional strategies that have statistically significant effects on student achievement.

Marzano and his colleagues offered a quote from researcher John Hattie as saying, "The most powerful single modification that enhances achievement is feedback" (Marzano et al., 2001, p. 96).

Further support for the use of formative assessment in both the learner-centered and knowledge-centered classrooms is provided by the National Research Council: "An important feature of the assessment-centered class-room is assessment that supports learning by providing students with oppor-tunities to review and improve their thinking" (NRC, 2005, p. 16).

The National Science Teachers Association offered a number of research-based position statements that describe the organization's stand on critical issues related to science education, including the role of assessment. The position statements help to guide administrators and teachers in the design and implementation of a curriculum that addresses important science goals and standards. The position statements can be viewed at http://www.nsta.org/position.

CREATING A VISION FOR FORMATIVE ASSESSMENT

There is a body of firm evidence that formative assessment is an essential component of classroom work and that its development can raise stan-dards of achievement. We know of no other way of raising standards for which such a strong prima facie case can be made. Our plea is that national and state policy makers will grasp this opportunity and take the lead in this direction.

—Black & Wiliam, 1998 (p. 147)

In an ideal world, all students would learn and be successful. Educators are well aware that there are many variables that influence student achievement. Yet many of the significant variables that determine what students will learn and how students will learn operate within the class-room setting. With the abundance of research on effective teaching and formative assessment, we know with certainty that the teacher is the key to student learning and that formative assessment is a powerful tool for promoting higher achievement.

In that teaching and assessment are so closely intertwined, the journey toward the use of formative assessment as a tool for increasing student achievement requires us to think critically and thoughtfully about each of these important issues.

- Schoolwide and personal beliefs and practices related to learning and assessment

- Traditional versus student-centered views of teaching and assessment
- Characteristics of effective formative assessment programs

■ EXAMINING BELIEFS AND PRACTICES

Our beliefs strongly influence our practices. There are understandings and misunderstandings associated with the term "assessment." The ways that teachers view student learning and their beliefs about the purposes of assessment will determine, to a great extent, how they teach and assess in their classrooms.

Clarifying beliefs and practices related to assessment is a first step in creating a vision for the design and implementation of formative assessment tools and strategies in the classroom. Black and Wiliam (1998) contend that the most important difficulties with assessment revolve around three issues: effective learning, a negative impact on learning, and managerial role of assessment. Reflection on these categories provides insight into how beliefs influence practice and help to identify areas in need of change.

An inventory for self-assessment and reflection of issues and practices related to effective learning, impact on learning, and the role of assessment is offered in Figure 1.2. Note the practices that *support* effective teaching and learning are listed under each category.

The chart may be useful for identifying one or more areas for which more information or consideration is needed or for identifying areas needing improvement at the district, school, or classroom level.

■ TRADITIONAL VERSUS STUDENT-CENTERED VIEWS OF ASSESSMENT

Another way to think about assessment is to compare the types of data and information that are collected and communicated in traditional and student-centered classrooms. For this comparison, information about student learning is compared to a photo album. Each way of collecting evidence of what students know and are able to do is one "photograph" in the album.

Two photo albums are shown. Picturing Student Achievement I in Figure 1.3 shows traditional ways that learning is assessed and communicated to students.

Picturing Student Achievement II in Figure 1.4 shows a variety of ways that information about student learning can be collected, communicated to students, and used to inform and guide instruction toward enhanced learning and higher achievement.

Two albums are provided to show a difference in beliefs about assessment. The first photo album implies that instruction and assessment are separate components where students are "taught" a lesson or series of lessons and then given tests to determine what they have learned. Generally, the test is the final measure of learning for a topic or unit.

Figure 1.2 An Inventory of Issues and Practices			
Issues and Practices Related to Effective Learning	*Agree*	*Disagree*	*Unsure*
Classroom assessments mostly discourage rote and superficial learning and focus on understanding			
Test items and methods of assessing in our school or district are consistent and shared among teachers			
There is consistency and clarity about what concepts and skills individually designed teacher-made tests actually assess			
Most teacher-made tests are criterion-referenced and reflect important goals and standards for the subject area			
Quality of work is emphasized over the quantity of work			
Issues and Practices Related to Impact on Learning	*Agree*	*Disagree*	*Unsure*
Providing useful feedback and giving suggestions for learning are emphasized over giving grades			
Competition with oneself for personal and continuous improvement is valued over competition between students			
Assessment feedback helps low-achieving students gain confidence in their ability to learn			
Issues and Practices Related to the Role of Assessment	*Agree*	*Disagree*	*Unsure*
Feedback to students serves a learning function as opposed to social and managerial functions			
Unlike external tests, teacher-developed assessments help inform teachers and students about strengths and weaknesses			
The analysis of students' work for purposes of motivation and improvement has a higher priority than a collection of grades			
Attention is given to the assessment records from previous grade levels			

In this view of assessment, student learning is determined and communicated by summative measures such as test scores and written reports identifying strengths and weaknesses that are translated into grades. Grades may also be affected by missing assignments, homework, and behavior.

Test scores alone do not represent the broad range of student learning, nor do they provide varied ways for students to show learning. For example, standardized and teacher-made tests often do not assess concept understanding beyond the knowledge or comprehension levels, process, thinking, or problem-solving skills, habits of mind, or the student's ability to apply concepts to technology and society.

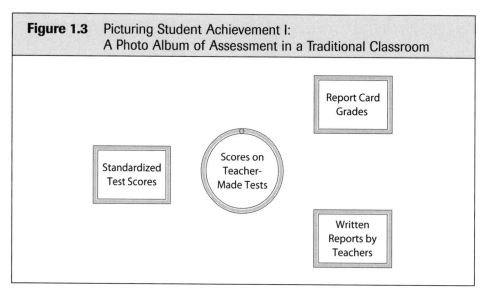

Figure 1.3   Picturing Student Achievement I:
A Photo Album of Assessment in a Traditional Classroom

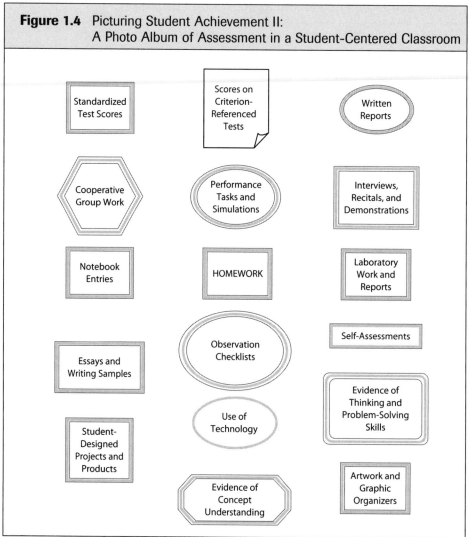

Figure 1.4   Picturing Student Achievement II:
A Photo Album of Assessment in a Student-Centered Classroom

The second photo album shows a very different view of student learning. This perspective shows that while scores on standardized and criterion-referenced tests and written reports may not go away as measures of achievement, a more complete description of learning can be compiled and communicated to students and others through a variety of formative assessments.

In this view of assessment, student work, demonstrations of learning, self-assessments, performances, and so forth are regarded as evidence of the extent to which learning goals were achieved. The assessment tools and strategies that expand this perspective of learning are embedded in instruction and used throughout the instructional process to inform students of their progress and to guide and enhance learning.

FORMATIVE ASSESSMENT ▪ AS "AUTHENTIC" ASSESSMENT

"Authentic assessment" is a term used by Wiggins in the early 1990s to describe assessments that are aligned with important learning goals and standards and are worth mastering. Authentic assessments emulate the standards that are set for those in professional fields and provide realistic contexts. Formative classroom assessments are authentic when they

- align with important goals and standards in the eight content categories of science
- are meaningful, purposeful, and instructional
- provide multiple and varied ways for students to show what they know and are able to do
- capture student thinking and mental constructs as well as their misunderstandings
- are thought-provoking and challenging
- provide opportunities for students to self-assess and take responsibility for learning

When built into the instructional plan, formative assessments provide immediate feedback about student learning without taking valuable time from instruction because they are part of instruction. For example, during an investigation, a teacher might use a checklist to record observations related to the safe and correct handling and use of equipment and the ability of students to work cooperatively in a group. Notebook entries may show that students have misinterpreted directions or misunderstood a concept or that students are on task and progressing well through the task. The key to successful formative assessment lies with the use of multiple and varied ways to capture evidence of thinking and learning that naturally flow from well-defined goals and rich and meaningful contexts for instruction.

■ CLEAR TARGETS FOR INSTRUCTION AND ASSESSMENT

Children develop theories about the world and how it works early in life. As learners, they continually link new information to prior knowledge and restructure their frames of thought. If we assess what we value, assessment tools must be appropriate for gathering the types of information about student learning that are aligned with clear instructional goals. Goals that are ill defined, taken for granted, assumed, or mistaken for instructional activities are seldom reached.

Goals for School Science

National and state leaders emphasize the need to view science as more than a set of accumulated facts and theories. The National Science Education Standards identified the goals for school science as educating students who are able to

- experience the richness and excitement of knowing about and understanding the natural world
- use appropriate scientific processes and principles in making personal decisions
- engage intelligently in public discourse and debate about matters of scientific and technological concern
- increase their economic productivity through the use of the knowledge, understanding, and skills of the scientifically literate person in their careers (NRC, 1996, p. 13)

Scientific Literacy

Scientific literacy is the goal of science education, but what does scientific literacy actually look like? Scientific literacy may be operationally defined by observing the behaviors of natural scientists, social scientists, behavioral scientists, and similar professional and amateur scientists.

Scientists by nature explore, investigate, and experiment to discover and uncover the mysteries of the universe and answer questions related to natural and social worlds. Although their methods are somewhat varied, they do have characteristics in common. There are similarities in the ways scientists formulate questions, generate hypotheses, make observations, collect and interpret data, check and recheck their findings, use what they learn to change their views of knowledge, ask new questions, and seek more answers.

Not surprisingly, these processes are common to problem solving in any discipline and to learning in general. The problems and issues faced by citizens in daily life are not unlike those faced by professionals and require practice of the same processes and thinking skills used by scientists, mathematicians, historians, artists, musicians, politicians, and so forth, to solve problems in their respective disciplines.

The National Science Education Standards (NRC, 1996) described a scientifically literate person as one who

- can ask, find, or determine answers to questions derived from curiosity about everyday experiences
- has the ability to describe, explain, and predict natural phenomena
- is able to read, with understanding, articles about science in the popular press and to engage in social conversation about the validity of the conclusions
- can identify scientific issues underlying national and local decisions and express positions that are scientifically and technologically informed
- is able to evaluate the quality of scientific information on the basis of its source and the methods used to generate it
- has the ability to pose and evaluate arguments based on evidence and to apply conclusions from such arguments appropriately
- is able to display scientific literacy by appropriately using technical terms and by applying concepts and processes (p. 22)

Science Content Categories

Underlying the characteristics of the scientifically literate citizen is a strong knowledge base, but as one can see from the description, the knowledge base alone is not the end product of science education. The instructional goals that are deemed most worthy of student learning in science are derived from the national and state standards projects that address the content categories identified in the National Science Education Standards (Figure 1.5) and are reflected in the Benchmarks for Science Literacy (American Association for the Advancement of Science [AAAS], 1993). It is critical for teachers to have a clear understanding of these important learning goals in order to guide students toward their mastery.

Steeped within this multidimensional view of science are opportunities for students to develop content-related skills and habits of mind, as well as other important twenty-first-century knowledge and learning skills such as

- information and media literacy
- communication skills
- complex thinking and reasoning
- problem solving, creativity
- interpersonal and collaborative skills
- self-direction, accountability and adaptability, and social responsibility. (Partnership for 21st Century Skills, http://www.21stcentury skills.org)

Science is an active process. If classroom science is to provide opportunities for students to learn and practice science as it exists throughout the scientific community, it must closely resemble the experiences and types of thinking commonly used by scientists in the field and laboratories of the world. The disciplines of science with their concepts and principles, topics, themes, problems, and issues offer the contexts through which knowledge and problem-solving skills, as well as skills of lifelong learning, can be

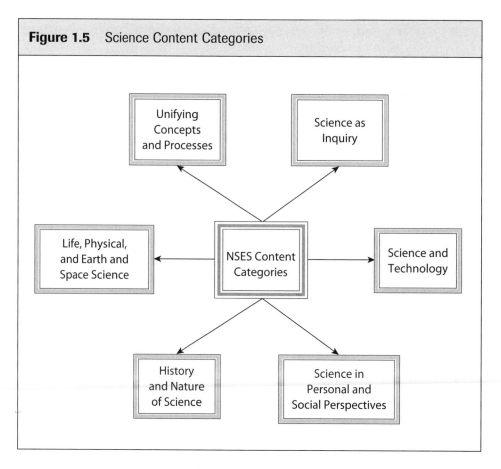

Figure 1.5 Science Content Categories

developed. National and state standards projects provide the focus for science curricula. Programs rich with developmentally appropriate inquiry-based experiences provide the basis for learning important concepts and developing skills and valued habits of mind.

Scientific Habits of Mind

Another important consideration on the road to the development of the well-informed citizenry is the development of habits of mind. This term refers to values and attitudes often called dispositions plus mathematical, logical, problem-solving and thinking skills, and communication and critical response skills valued by the scientific community and by society in general. Scientists exhibit these values, attitudes, and skills throughout their professional work and in their personal lives. Figure 1.6 shows a list of values, attitudes, and skills underlying science gleaned from national standards projects and the literature that are collectively referred to as habits of mind.

These qualities and characteristics described in the habits of mind can be developed in the science classroom. Teachers who are enthusiastic and model desired attitudes, values, and skills for lifelong learning strongly influence the attitudes and behaviors developed by students. When students are given opportunities to engage in inquiry-based science, they are able to develop and demonstrate the habits of mind.

Creating a vision for formative assessment as an approach to enhancing student learning in science requires an understanding of standards-

Figure 1.6 Scientific Habits of Mind

Habits of Mind	Descriptions
Honesty	Truthful and trustworthy; free from deceit; exhibits accuracy in reporting data or information
Curiosity and a Desire for Knowledge	An innate or developed desire for knowing and understanding the world
Cooperation	A shared discussion of ideas, theories, and techniques at the local, state, national, and international levels
Having Confidence in and Relying on Data	Respecting evidence, which also implies the testing and retesting of ideas and monitoring of one's own thinking processes
Comfort With Ambiguity	The results of science are always tentative; testing and retesting provide more confidence in one's conclusions; ambiguity gives rise to new problems and questions
Balancing Open-Mindedness With Skepticism	Being open to new theories and willingness to disregard current ones; respecting new ideas and proposals, but remaining skeptical until evidence is offered
Respect for Living Things	All living things deserve human care both in the lab and in the field; attitudes and behaviors in the handling and care of live organisms says much about our value systems as human beings
Willingness to Modify Explanations	Newly acquired data or reinterpretations of existing data may require one to modify explanations for phenomena and events; willingness to rethink conclusions is often one of science's and science learning's most difficult personal decisions
Respecting and Trusting the Thinking Process	Science is an active process defined by patterns of reasoning that lead to theory building and theory testing; trust in the process is an essential element
Computation and Estimation	Ability to solve mathematical problems in real-world situations; the ability to explain how to calculate an answer before carrying it out; ability to express arguments quantitatively
Manipulation and Observation	Using first-hand, sensory experiences and tools of technology for learning and problem solving
Critical-Response Skills	Ability to separate "sense" from "nonsense" when confronted with claims put forth by experts and non-experts about products, systems or devices, and health and welfare; ability to make judgments based on the character of an assertion

related instructional goals as well as an understanding of the purpose, strategies, and tools of formative assessment. The following chapters are intended to provide greater insight into ways formative assessment can be used to enhance learning in science.

2

Using Rubrics to Guide Learning

THE WHAT AND WHY OF RUBRICS ■

What Are They?

In earlier times, the term "rubric" referred to a title or heading of a law, custom, or rule of procedure written in red lettering which signified its importance. As discipline-specific standards were gaining prominence throughout the 1990s and beyond, rubrics were introduced in education as ways for teachers to identify and communicate important dimensions of learning (Burke, 2006; Enger & Yager, 2001; Hammerman & Musial, 2008; Lantz, 2004; Stiggins, 1994; Wiggins, 1992).

The term *rubric* sometimes means different things to different people. In a general sense, rubrics can be thought of as a set of criteria or rules that provides direction in determining what students know and are able to do.

Why Do We Use Them?

Rubrics provide teachers with new ways of viewing learning goals and new ways of assessing student work. Rubrics enable teachers to abandon subjective evaluation methods and replace them with carefully constructed instruments that communicate more clearly expectations for learning, and to identify students' strengths and weaknesses related to important learning goals. The key to the successful use of rubrics is the extent to which they reflect what students need to become informed citizens in the global community.

What Do They Look Like?

In their simplest form, rubrics may be an answer key for a multiple-choice test. In this case, the criteria are the correct answers and the rule is to count the number of correct answers and perhaps cluster them into different subtest scores. Rubrics for multiple-choice tests are simple. Rubrics used to describe performance tasks and products require more thought and consideration. Rubrics that identify criteria for complex performance tasks and products are one of three forms: holistic, generalized, or analytic.

■ HOLISTIC RUBRICS

What Are They?

Has a friend ever recommended a movie or a book because he or she thought it was "great"? Comments such as "don't miss this one," "you're going to love it," or "one of the best of the year," provide an overall rating based on a large number of variables that are important to the viewer or reader. In this case, the friend is sharing a critique based on his or her standards for excellence.

In education, holistic rubrics generally consist of sets of criteria that define various levels of achievement. They are used for judging products and performances in their entirety. A holistic rubric requires the assessor to consider a product or performance as a single entity or construct and to determine the "best fit" to one of the levels described in the rubric.

Why Do We Use Them?

Advocates of holistic scoring rubrics contend that when products and performances are considered in terms of discrete pieces or indicators, the assessor may be distracted from appreciating the beauty and continuity of the product or performance as a whole. The holistic approach enables the observer to not only look for expected indicators, but also identify and respond to unique features of the product or performance, factors that may not be considered with other types of rubrics.

What Do They Look Like?

You have seen examples of holistic scoring. Think about the last time you observed Olympic-level sport competitions such as gymnastics or figure skating. For each performance, a numerical score is given based on the quality of the performance as measured against a standard. Often there are several judges awarding scores, and these scores are averaged. The judges evaluate the total performance, considering the required components as well as those elements that make the performance exceptional or outstanding. These elements may not be predetermined but may enter into the final score for the performance.

HOLISTIC RUBRIC FOR A SCIENCE REPORT

At the school science fair there was much excitement and celebration as students displayed and presented projects related to science topics and standards they had been researching and studying. They began their projects by asking inquiry questions and identifying a variety of experiences and investigations they would use to answer their questions. Their involvement in the projects enabled them to take responsibility for their learning and to become "experts" in a field of interest to them.

As part of their project, students were required to submit a written report identifying and describing both processes and products. Through their presentations and reports, students demonstrated an understanding of the science concepts they investigated, the processes they used to answer their inquiry questions, the data they collected, the reasoning behind their conclusions, and the applications and implications of their research.

Their teacher, Mr. Williams, provided the predesigned holistic rubric shown to guide the students in planning their projects and in writing their reports. The holistic rubric was then used to assess and score the reports.

SCIENCE REPORT RUBRIC

4—Exceptional: The report includes a review of research, identifies a rationale for the project, and gives a clear and concise explanation of the project. An inquiry question is identified, and the design of the project is appropriate and shows originality and creativity. The scientific processes used throughout the project are used with precision. Data are displayed, and other visuals, such as pictures or drawings, are precise and creatively used to describe changes or to explain phenomena. A reasonable conclusion is drawn, and the report shows that the student made sense of the learning. There is a very good explanation of the applications or implications of the research. Overall, the report is well organized, containing sufficient to exceptional detail, examples, descriptions, and insights. Unique or unexpected features of the overall performance will be considered for this rating.

3—Meets Standards/On Target: The report includes an acceptable review of research and identifies a rationale. Explanation of the project is clear and detailed. Inquiry question is identified, and design is appropriate and original. Scientific processes are appropriate for the project and are mostly used with precision. Data are displayed, and some visuals are used to describe changes or explain phenomena. Conclusion is reasonable and sensible. Applications or implications are acceptable. Overall, the report is well organized and acceptable in detail, examples, descriptions, and insights.

(Continued)

(Continued)

> *2—Lacking:* The report includes a minimal review of research and a weak rationale for the project. The explanation of the project lacks clarity but includes some detail. Inquiry question is identified, and the design is appropriate but lacking in originality. Processes are mostly appropriate and precise. Data are shown, but visuals are weak or lacking. Conclusion is weak or does not follow from data. Applications or implications are few or lacking. Overall, the report is somewhat organized but is weak in detail, examples, descriptions, and insights. Report minimally shows what student learned.
>
> *1—Inadequate:* The report does not include a review of research, or review is minimal. Rationale is lacking. The explanation of the project is weak or lacking. The design of the project does not address the inquiry question well. Processes are inappropriate or appropriate but not precise. Data are discrepant or lacking, and visuals are lacking or inappropriate. The conclusion does not follow from the data, and little sense is made of the findings. Overall, the report is not well organized, nor does it contain sufficient details, examples, descriptions, and insights to show that learning has occurred.

Limitations to Holistic Scoring

The holistic rubric identifies components of an exemplary report and offers opportunities for unexpected or creative features to be considered in the rating. But, in spite of the best efforts to describe the levels of performance in a predesigned holistic rubric, there will be some products or performances that do not "fit" the descriptions, requiring some degree of subjectivity to enter into the assessment process.

Holistic rubrics do not enable teachers and students to diagnose specific strengths or weaknesses. "You will never be able to help students understand and learn to replicate the fine details of sound performance by teaching them to score holistically" (Stiggins, 1994, p. 194). Over time, additional performances that represent the salient characteristics of each of the four groups may be selected and used to add clarity to the categories of the rubric.

■ DESIGNING HOLISTIC RUBRICS

One approach to developing holistic rubrics is to focus on the performance rather than on predesigned rubrics. In this approach, teachers spend more time and effort developing rich performance tasks than designing the tasks to match predesigned rubrics. Such performances are designed to reflect the knowledge and skills exhibited by professionals in the field. Student performances are then analyzed to determine the extent to which they measure up to a standard. The characteristics of various levels of performance are identified and are used to describe the rubric in the future. Figure 2.1 shows these steps for designing holistic rubrics in this way.

Figure 2.1   Designing Holistic Rubrics

One approach to designing holistic rubrics is to:

1. identify or design a performance task that addresses standards and reflects the high quality of work characteristic of professionals in the field;

2. have students perform the task;

3. view the performances in their entirety;

4. compare the work to the standards, and separate performances into two groups: those that **meet the standard**s, and those that **do not meet the standards;**

5. consider the performances that **meet the standards** and select a subgroup that stands out as **exceptional**;

6. review the performances that did not meet the standards, and separate them into two subgroups: those performances that are minimally l**acking or weak** in some components, and those that are **seriously inadequate; and finally,**

7. return to each of the four groups, ranging from seriously inadequate to exceptional, and identify the characteristics within the student work or performance that best describe each category or group.

These descriptions constitute the final rubric that can be used to score other student work on the same performance.

GENERALIZED RUBRICS   ■

What Are They?

Some experts contend that the disciplines are innately interconnected through similar dimensions, and therefore, generalized statements can be written that relate to a variety of performances within the same discipline or across disciplines. Generalized scoring rubrics provide a framework for assessing a task without explicitly identifying discrete indicators.

Why Do We Use Them?

Because the levels of performance are described in general terms, these rubrics can be used to assess a variety of tasks in a variety of disciplines. They do not identify specifically what students know, but provide a more general description of their performance levels for a set of indicators of learning. Generalized rubrics enable teachers and students to measure a performance qualitatively and quantitatively, but they are lacking in precision.

What Do They Look Like?

In a generalized rubric, important categories of indicators of learning are identified. For each of the categories and the indicators, if identified, the rubric describes various performance levels that best match the student work or performance.

■ EXAMPLES OF GENERALIZED RUBRICS

For a generalized rubric to be useful, the assignment, project, or performance must include components of the categories of learning identified in the rubric. The categories of content, skills, and habits of mind may be further defined by specific indicators, but that is not always the case in generalized rubrics. Figure 2.2 shows a generalized rubric in its simplest form. In this example there are four levels of performance related to the three categories: concept understanding, use of process skills, and use of communication skills.

Figure 2.2   A Simple Generalized Rubric

Concept Understanding

3   Demonstrates a complete understanding of important concepts or ideas

2   Displays an adequate understanding of important concepts or ideas

1   Displays an incomplete understanding of important concepts and ideas

0   Demonstrates serious misconceptions about concepts and ideas

Process Skills

3   Demonstrates mastery of important strategies and skills

2   Demonstrates important strategies and skills independently without significant error

1   Demonstrates important strategies and skills with guidance

0   Makes critical errors when carrying out important strategies and skills

Communication Skills

3   Consistently and effectively communicates by providing a clear main idea with support and elaboration

2   Communicates information by providing a clear main idea with little detail

1   Intermittently communicates a clear main idea

0   Rarely communicates a clear main ide

The generalized rubric in Figure 2.3 shows specific indicators of learning in one category of learning and a slightly more precise description of each of the other three categories. Three performance levels are shown with explanations that differentiate them. For each of the categories, the teacher or students select the performance level that best represents the student work or performance. The four categories of learning represented in this rubric are

1. *the understanding of concepts and principles,* including the use of terminology, the quality and accuracy of explanations, and the quality and accuracy of representations (data tables, charts, graphs, graphic organizers, or other);

2. *the understanding and use of skills and strategies for learning,* including inquiry, process and thinking skills, problem-solving, communicating, and accessing and using information;

3. *the use of tools and technologies,* including manipulative materials such as magnifiers and microscopes, equipment for finding mass, volume, and distance, thermometers and calculators, A/V equipment, computers, and other resources; and

4. *evidence of connections and meaningful applications of learning* to technology, society, lives of students, and national, state, or important issues.

In a generalized rubric, the indicators of learning and the descriptions for each category are, in fact, "general" in nature. There is still an element of subjectivity in the analysis and scoring of the student work since the descriptions are not specific to what is expected in the product or performance.

In some ways the generalized rubric resembles a holistic rubric in that some indicators have multiple components, such as "the understanding and use of skills and strategies for learning." The more complex the category of learning is, the less likely the student work or performance will match with the descriptions in the three performance levels. In this case, the best one can do is to select the category of "best fit."

Figure 2.3   A Detailed Generalized Rubric

Indicators of Learning	Meets Standards	Approaches Standards	Not Yet
Understanding of Concepts and Principles • Uses of terminology • Explanations with reasoning • Representations	Uses all terminology appropriately Gives accurate and clear explanations with support Shows data and thought through good use of graphics	Uses some or most terminology; some used inappropriately Uses incomplete or weak explanations or describes misconceptions Uses some graphics to show data or thought	Uses little or no terminology or inappropriate terminology to describe or explain Uses faulty or inappropriate explanations; little/no understanding Uses few or no graphics or uses graphics inappropriately

(Continued)

Figure 2.3   (Continued)

Indicators of Learning	Meets Standards	Approaches Standards	Not Yet
Understanding and use of skills and strategies	Shows good understanding and use of skills and strategies Shows appropriate use of most skills with no errors	Shows some understanding and use of skills and strategies Uses some skills and strategies inappropriately or with errors	Shows little or no understanding or use of skills and strategies Shows inappropriate use of all or most skills, with many significant errors
Use of tools and other technologies	Makes good use of tools and technology Uses all appropriately	Uses some tools and technology Uses most or all appropriately	Uses few or no tools or technologies Shows inappropriate use
Identification of relevant applications and connections to technology, society, personal lives, or important issues	Identifies and explains several ways concepts and principles apply or connect Provides relevant examples with detail	Identifies one way that concepts and principles apply or connect Provides one relevant example with minimum detail	Identifies one or no ways concepts and principles apply or connect to technology, society, personal lives, or issues Lacks detail

■ ANALYTIC RUBRICS

What Are They?

We use analytic rubrics in our everyday lives to assess the qualities and characteristics of many things with which we come in contact. For example, it is not unusual to assess the quality of a restaurant based on such factors as friendliness of staff, cleanliness, quality of food, quantity of food, and value. Often aesthetics and emotional responses influence our assessments, as well.

In an analytic system, the standards and the indicators of learning that define them are identified and considered separately. The identification of specific indicators inherent in products or performance tasks allows teachers and students to assess concept understanding, process, thinking and learning skills, and habits of mind as separate components. This discrete approach produces analytic rubrics.

Why Do We Use Them?

Analytic rubrics focus attention on important learning goals and enable teachers and students to measure the extent to which the goals are mastered. Analytic rubrics are less subjective than generalized or holistic rubrics because they consider each indicator of learning objectively. "Analytical rubrics provide ongoing assessment that is integrated with instruction in a continuous feedback loop that allows teachers to refocus instruction on an ongoing basis" (Burke, 2006, p. 132).

Here the performance is not considered in its entirely. One might question whether the whole product or performance is equal in value to the sum of the parts. Sometimes it is, but sometimes it is not. When the specific standards of quality are itemized, subjective qualities that elicit emotional responses are lacking and valued unexpected or creative features are overlooked.

However, the analytic rubric does provide for more objective and specific feedback to students for each of the task-specific indicators of learning. The analytic rubric provides a way for students to self-assess and identify their strengths and weaknesses in terms of specific goal-related indicators of learning.

What Do They Look Like?

In planning instruction, teachers consider what aspects of their instructional goals are most important and need to be monitored throughout instruction so that students have the best chance of mastering them. To do this, they identify the important concepts and skills, and habits of mind and identify them as "indicators of learning."

Instructional activities are selected or designed to provide opportunities for students to show evidence of learning for each indicator. The teacher, often with the help of students, adds a scale such as "right on" and "not yet" if evidence of learning is either present or not present, or a scale with more levels of performance such as "complete," "almost," and "not yet" if there are several degrees of performance. There may be as many as four or five levels of performance, but if so, each level must have a clear and distinctive description to minimize subjectivity in scoring the work. In every case, one end of the scale must show that the indicator of learning was exhibited at the highest level of expectation, and the other end must show that the indicator of learning was not attempted or shown. For example, for the indicator "the inquiry question is testable," there are only two performance levels, since the question is either testable or not.

ASSESSMENT TASKS ■
WITH ANALYTIC RUBRICS

Analytic rubrics may be used to assess simple tasks that provide immediate feedback about learning. Shown here are two tasks that assess concepts and skills that students learned as part of a unit on Weather and Climate. Note that in each case the indicators of learning link directly to the learning goals.

ASSESSMENT TASKS FOR A UNIT ON CLIMATE

1. Reading and Interpreting a Data Table

INSTRUCTIONAL GOAL: The student will be able to read and interpret data from a variety of sources.

TASK: Use the information provided on the data table to answer the questions.

DATA: Average Yearly Temperature and Rainfall for Riverside, California

	Jan.	Feb.	March	April	May	June	July	Aug.	Sept.	Oct.	Nov.	Dec.
Temp °F	51	53	55	60	65	69.5	80.5	80	73	63.5	58	53
Rainfall in inches	1.81	2.58	2	0.91	0.18	0.04	0.01	0.20	0.11	0.60	0.87	2.65

QUESTIONS

1. During which month is the temperature the

   a. highest? _____   b. lowest? _____

2. During which month is the amount of precipitation the

   a. highest? _____   b. lowest? _____

3. What was the average rainfall for the summer months of June, July, and August?

4. What is the median temperature for the year?

ANALYTIC RUBRIC FOR READING AND INTERPRETING A DATA TABLE

Indicators of Learning		
The student read and interpreted data from a table to	*Right on*	*Not yet*
Identify the months with the highest and lowest temperatures (July; January)		
Identify the months with the highest and lowest amounts of precipitation (March; July)		
Calculate the average rainfall for June, July, Aug (0.08 inches)		
Determine the median temperature (63.5 °F)		

2. Constructing a Climagraph

Climagraphs are a special type of graphs on which data from temperature and rainfall are plotted.

INSTRUCTIONAL GOAL: The student will be able to access and use data to construct a climagraph

TASK: Plot the data from the data table for Raleigh, North Carolina, on the graph below. Make a bar graph for the rainfall data and a line graph for the for the temperature data.

CLIMAGRAPH FOR RALEIGH, NORTH CAROLINA

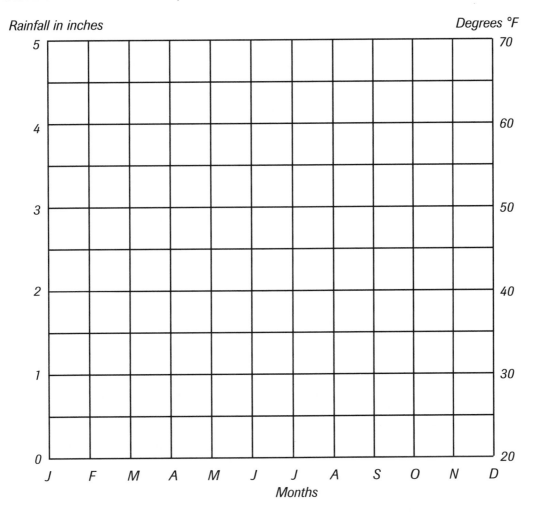

Average temperature and rainfall for Raleigh, NC, for the years 1931–1995

	Jan.	Feb.	March	April	May	June	July	Aug.	Sept.	Oct.	Nov.	Dec.
Temp °F	40.5	43.3	51.8	60.1	67.8	74.7	78.0	77.4	71.8	61.0	52.3	43.9
Rainfall in inches	3.7	3.5	4.0	3.0	4.2	4.2	5.3	4.5	3.4	3.1	3.0	3.2

(Continued)

(Continued)

ANALYTIC RUBRIC FOR CONSTRUCTING A CLIMAGRAPH

Indicators of Learning			
The student accessed and used information to correctly:	*Got it*	*Almost*	*Not yet*
Plot temperature data on a graph	All data points are accurate	Some data points are accurate	Few/no data points are accurate
Display temperature data on a line graph	Data are shown on a well-constructed line graph	Data are poorly displayed or graph is poorly constructed	Data are not displayed or graph is inappropriate
Plot rainfall data on a graph	Rainfall data are correctly plotted	Some data points are accurate	Few/no data points are accurate
Display rainfall data on a bar graph	Data are shown on a well-constructed bar graph	Data are poorly displayed or graph is poorly constructed	Data are not displayed or graph is inappropriate

■ DESIGNING ANALYTIC RUBRICS

Identifying the features or characteristics of a product or performance that are worthy of assessing is the first step in designing an analytic rubric. These indicators of learning should be linked to important educational goals and be considered important for students to learn. Indicators related to the understanding of concepts and the development of contextual learning skills, thinking skills, communication skills, and valued habits of mind define a standard for learning and should be included in the rubric.

Rubrics for Fun

An activity is provided for those teachers who are not familiar with analytic rubrics or have not developed task-specific rubrics for use in their classrooms. The context of the activity is one in which many people might consider themselves "experts"—chocolate chip cookies. In this example, the indicators of "excellence" are determined by the experts—you!

By putting the activity in a familiar context, it is possible to focus on two important factors related to the development and use of rubrics: (1) standards and indicators of high quality may vary among groups of people and (2) even with an identified set of indicators for "excellence," there may be differences in the ratings of products.

THE GREATEST CHOCOLATE CHIP COOKIE

OVERVIEW: This activity will take you through a four-step process for designing an analytic rubric for a familiar and much-loved product. Chocolate chip cookies are a favorite treat of both children and adults. There are many recipes for making these delectable creations at home and many familiar brands that are offered commercially.

GOAL: To determine what makes a chocolate chip cookie a *great* chocolate chip cookie.

INSTRUCTIONAL OBJECTIVES: The learner will describe the qualities and characteristics of great chocolate chip cookies and use these as indicators to create an analytic rubric.

Part I: Creating an Analytic Rubric
for Chocolate Chip Cookies

1. With a partner, identify and list at least four to five characteristics of great chocolate chip cookies. You are considered the "experts" and set the standards for excellence.

   - _____

   - _____

   - _____

   - _____

   - _____

2. Share your characteristics with another team. Identify similarities and differences in the characteristics you chose. You may add to or modify your list of characteristics, if you wish.

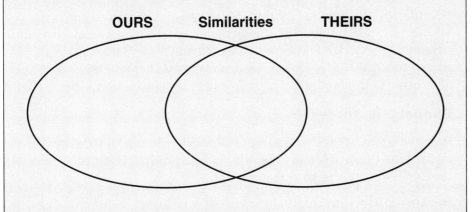

OURS   **Similarities**   **THEIRS**

(Continued)

(Continued)

3. Write your characteristics in the vertical column of the rubric labeled "Characteristics of GREAT chocolate chip cookies."
4. Next, consider at least three or four levels for rating each of the characteristics. Write a short but clear description for each of the ratings and assign a numerical score for each. For example, if you have four levels, such as GREAT, Pretty Good, So/So, and NOT, you might assign the highest category a 3 and the others 2, 1, and 0. Write your categories and descriptions in the boxes at the top of the rubric

RUBRIC FOR CHOCOLATE CHIP COOKIES

Categories for Rating Cookies

Characteristics of GREAT Chocolate Chip Cookies				

Part II: Applying the Rubric

Because there are no set standards for great chocolate chip cookies, you have created a rubric for chocolate chip cookies based on your personal knowledge and experiences. Now, you will use the rubric to assess chocolate chip cookies to determine which one or ones measure up to your standards.

PRODUCT ASSESSMENT

INSTRUCTIONAL OBJECTIVES: The learners will describe the use of an analytic rubric to assess the quality of a product and describe its usefulness as a decision-making tool.

INQUIRY QUESTION: How do various brands or types of chocolate chip cookies compare to the standards we have identified?

BACKGROUND INFORMATION: Chocolate chip cookies can be made at home or purchased at bakeries or other locations such as airports and shopping malls. They are also commercially produced and available at grocery stores. The quality of these products varies greatly, and some may or may not measure up to identified standards.

Product testing is a process by which we compare products to a standard or set of standards that we value. Product testing provides a way of classifying products and communicating the degree to which the products match those standards.

MATERIALS: balances and mass sets; measuring tapes; dissecting tools; paper towels; a variety of chocolate chip cookies, both commercially produced and homemade, if possible.

ENGAGEMENT: Although chocolate chip cookies are popular, not all brands and types meet the high standards of being a "great chocolate chip cookie." In this activity, you will use the rubric you created to assess a variety of chocolate chip cookies to determine how well different chocolate chip cookies measure up to the standards you identified in your rubric.

EXPLORATION: You will be given chocolate chip cookies to analyze and assess.

1. Each group should assign the same number or product name to each of the cookies for purposes of comparison and record it on the data table.
2. Task: Using any or all of the materials provided, analyze each cookie to determine how it measures up to each of your characteristics of great cookies. You may use any or all of the materials to help in your analysis of the characteristics you identified in your rubric. Write a description of the characteristics of each cookie on the data table.
3. Using your rubric, rate each cookie on each of the characteristics, and assign a score for each cookie. Order your cookies from the one with the highest rating to the one with the lowest for meeting your standards.

DATA TABLE

Cookie # or Name	Description of Cookie	Rating

(Continued)

(Continued)

EXPLANATION: Share ideas and insights about your investigation in a large group or small groups.

1. Describe your findings. Which brand or type of cookie received the highest rating? Compare your results with those of other groups. Identify similarities and differences.
2. Explain the processes you used to determine a rating for each characteristic.
3. Do you think the processes you used provided accurate information about the quality of the cookies? What would you do differently the next time, if anything?
4. Were some characteristics more difficult to assess than others? Why or why not?
5. What characteristic (if any) was most important to your group?
6. Was the number of performance levels you created sufficient for the task? What would it be like if there were too few? What would it be like if there were too many?
7. Did the members of your group agree on the rating for each of the cookies? Was there some disagreement? If so, describe.
8. Overall, describe your level of satisfaction with the rubric, the tests, and the outcome.

EVALUATION: Assessing the rubric

- How well did the characteristics of the cookies you were given match the descriptions of the rating categories you designed on your rubric?
- What changes (if any) would you make in the rubric if you were going to rate these or other brands or types of chocolate chip cookies?

APPLICATION TO CLASSROOM ASSESSMENT: Describe how analytic rubrics can be used to provide feedback to students about their progress in meeting educational goals and performance standards.

ELABORATION: What additional information do you need to know to be able to design and use analytic rubrics in your classroom?

■ RUBRICS FOR SELF-ASSESSMENT AND PEER ASSESSMENT

Often students are given assignments with a set of directions and left on their own to interpret what is expected. In this traditional approach, students complete their assignments and submit their work, which is often done to the best of their abilities, to their teacher. In return, they receive a score or grade on the assignment. Students may be delighted with minimal feedback if they received a high score, or they may be totally confused as to why they received a score or grade lower than what they expected. Without specific feedback related to their work, students are left to infer that the assignment did not "measure up" to what was expected by the teacher. In such cases, it is not clear whether the students understood what they were expected to show or do or whether they did not have the knowledge or skills to show or do it.

In a student-centered classroom, rubrics are used to identify and describe what important knowledge and skills "look like" in the context of an instructional unit. When shared with students, rubrics and models of high-quality work or exemplars clarify the expectations for assignments or projects. Rubrics not only define the instructional goals and performance standards, they enable teachers to provide feedback to students about their progress in meeting them. Through constructive feedback, students can focus on specific knowledge or skills that need improvement.

Black and Wiliam (1998) contend that "if formative assessment is to be productive, pupils should be trained in self-assessment so that they can understand the main purposes of their learning and thereby grasp what they need to do to achieve" (p. 144). Rubrics can be used by students to self-assess. As students work through an assignment, they can compare their work to the descriptions given for each indicator of learning and determine how well their work matches the descriptions. Students may find it useful to review their work with a peer who will offer a second opinion about the quality of the work, share ideas and insights, and make suggestions for improvement.

It is important to remember that in formative assessment, student work is not scored for purposes of reporting to others. Rather, it is scored with the purpose of providing information to teachers and providing feedback to students about their learning. Examples of analytic rubrics will be shown throughout this book.

DESIGN A RUBRIC ■

Design a holistic, generalized, or analytic rubric for a project or assignment you give to your students. Use the rubric and note student reactions. Analyze and evaluate the rubric in terms of its ability to provide each of these dimensions.

- clarity of expectations
- guidance to students as they worked through the task
- feedback to students related to their progress
- a way for students to self-assess
- information about areas of learning that need improvement

3

Observation Checklists and Effective Questioning

OBSERVATION CHECKLISTS ■

What Are They?

Observation checklists are one means of recording evidence of performance and learning throughout the instructional process. As tools for formative assessment, checklists provide a way to record aspects of learning, including concept understanding, skill development, valued behaviors, and habits of mind that are observed in the classroom.

Why Do We Use Them?

Checklists may be designed to record concept understanding through discussion or oral presentations, but because observations are sporadic and somewhat subjective, checklists may be better suited to assessing behaviors and skills that are valued in the classroom. Observation checklists are a quick and easy way to take note of dispositions, study habits, social skills, communication skills, and problem-solving skills. The notations generally include the date of the observations and a positive or negative response and may include space for written comments.

When shared with students, the notations provide feedback that either reinforces positive behavior or calls attention to behaviors that need to be modified, developed further, or changed. Observation checklists are useful for determining, among other things, if students are

- on task, doing quality work, and making progress
- able to apply skills of inquiry and other contextual learning skills
- displaying dispositions and other habits of mind
- working cooperatively/collaboratively
- practicing safety and carefully handling equipment
- selecting and using equipment wisely
- taking responsibility for roles or actions
- engaging in meaningful discussion with others

What Do They Look Like?

There are many ways to design checklists. A single checklist may be used to record information for one student or for an entire class. It may deal with only a few or many important aspects of behavior and learning. What is most important is that the checklist is user-friendly and capable of providing information that is meaningful and related to effective teaching and learning.

■ SAMPLE OBSERVATION CHECKLISTS

Checklists for Individual Students

Dispositions that underlie science and are a subcategory of habits of mind might be noted using a checklist such as the one shown in Figure 3.1. In this

Figure 3.1   A Checklist for Assessing Dispositions

Disposition	Date/Comments	Date/Comments	Date/Comments	Date/Comments
Curiosity and a Desire for Knowledge				
Cooperation				
Having Confidence in and Relying on Data				
Comfort With Ambiguity				
Respect for Living Things				
Willingness to Modify Explanations				
Respecting and Trusting the Thinking Process				

example, the observer would note the dates a behavior related to the disposition was observed and add comments to describe or explain the situation or condition.

Figure 3.2 shows a checklist for recording observations of classroom behaviors and practices that are considered important in a student-centered classroom. Behaviors are identified along with their characteristics and space to record the dates observed and comments. Notations should be shared and discussed with students periodically. The checklists may also be useful for providing information to parents about student behaviors, work habits, and learning.

Figure 3.2	Checklist for Assessing Classroom Behaviors							
Behavior	*Characteristic*	*Dates Observed*						*Comments*
Timeliness	In place on time							
	Class and homework are on time							
Organization	Keeps notebook up-to-date and neat							
	Comes prepared for class							
	Good quality of class work and homework							
Effort	Works consistently							
	Analyzes and corrects errors							
	Takes pride in work							
	Is honest and trustworthy							
	Shows persistence							
Involvement	Participates actively							
	Works well in a group							
	Assists others when needed							
	Shows respect for teacher and students							
	Shows respect for living things							
Skills	Applies skills of inquiry accurately							
	Shows evidence of critical thinking and problem solving							

Checklists for Groups

Checklists can be designed so that notations for a group or an entire class can be made on one or two pages. The checklist in Figure 3.3 identifies six behaviors that are important for safe and effective classrooms. This model is easier to manage but provides less space for recording dates of observations and comments.

Figure 3.3 Group Checklist for Safe and Effective Practices							
Name	Follows safety rules	Selects and uses equipment responsibly	Stays on task; uses time wisely	Accepts responsibility for roles and actions	Engages in meaningful discussion with peers	Completes work on time	Comments

EFFECTIVE QUESTIONING   ■

Discussions in which pupils are led to talk about their understanding in their own ways are important aids to increasing knowledge and improving understanding. Dialogue with the teacher provides the opportunity for the teacher to respond to and reorient a pupil's thinking.

—Black & Wiliam, 1998, p. 144

Weiss, Pasley, Smith, Banilower, and Heck (2003) identified the use of questioning strategies as an indicator of the high-quality classroom. As with all skills, teachers must practice the art of asking good questions in the context of science. Thought-provoking questions should be an integral part of the instructional plan to ensure that students have the opportunity to think critically and logically.

The use of questions throughout instruction is linked positively to increased student achievement (Marzano, Pickering, & Pollock, 2001). Asking questions that promote reflection on purpose and process and discussion of concepts and skills enables teachers to gain insight into student thinking and learning before, during, and after an investigation.

Through discussion, teachers can determine how instruction is perceived, received, and valued by students and assess the effectiveness of the instructional approach for developing concepts and skills and for reaching goals. Discussion can also identify stumbling blocks or barriers to learning that students might be experiencing, as well as misconceptions they may have developed.

QUESTIONS FOR THINKING   ■
AND PROBLEM SOLVING

When planning instruction, teachers should carefully consider the inquiry questions that are posed by students and focus instruction on questions that build deeper understandings of concepts and require greater complexity of thought over time. *The Taxonomy of Educational Objectives* (Bloom et al., 1956) provides a framework for the design of instruction at six levels of knowing and thinking. The levels range from basic recall of information to more complex levels of knowledge, thinking, and reasoning.

Although dated, the framework continues to be useful as a guide for designing questions with a range of complexity. Figure 3.4 shows the six levels of cognitive objectives and a brief description of each.

Educational objectives define the concepts and skills as well as the levels of thought that will be addressed through instruction and determine, in part, the types of questions that students will be able to discuss effectively. Questions that relate directly to instruction can be posed at all phases of instruction. The questions should not only provide the opportunity for students to reflect on and explain their learning, but they should also challenge their thinking.

Figure 3.5 shows examples of questions at the six levels of thought in the context of science that may be useful in planning instruction.

Figure 3.4 Bloom's Taxonomy of Educational Objectives	
Level	*Description*
Knowledge	• Recall specific facts and generalizations • Recall methods, processes, patterns, structures, and settings
Comprehension	• Know what is communicated and can use the material or idea without relating it • Interpret ideas and data • Make estimates or predictions based on conditions
Application	• Use abstractions correctly in new situations • Use principles, ideas, or methods to solve a problem
Analysis	• Make clear the relative hierarchy of ideas in material • Make explicit the relations among ideas • Identify patterns, parts, and messages
Synthesis	• Use previously established ideas to create something new, such as a plan, a product, or a process
Evaluation	• Make a judgment about the value of materials and methods used for particular purposes • Identify and evaluate differences between ideas, actions, or habits of mind

■ QUESTIONS FOR INSTRUCTION AND ASSESSMENT

Questions Throughout Instruction

Questions play an important role in all phases of instruction. The Five E's lesson plan format identifies five distinct phases for effective instruction—engage, explore, explain, elaborate, and evaluate—where questions can be used to promote thinking and capture evidence of thinking. The lesson plan may be used to design learning experiences for one day or several days.

There should be flexibility among and within phases of the model to allow for modification of the instructional plan, as data about student learning are collected through formative assessments and analyzed. Figure 3.6 identifies the phases, provides a short description of each, and describes how questions might be used to promote thinking at each phase.

Informal Questioning

Informal questioning may occur as students work through lab activities or investigations. Casual questions about process or concept understanding provide information to determine how students are progressing and if instructional objectives are being met. Feedback from questions can be used to guide students in their work or modify instruction, as needed.

Figure 3.5 Questions at Six Levels of Thought

Level of Thought	Questions
Knowledge: identification and recall of information; define terms; knowledge of criteria	• Who, what, when, where, how? • What is the definition of this term? • How would you use this piece of equipment? • Who invented the microscope?
Comprehension: organize or select facts or ideas; interpret ideas; translate—make estimates or predictions based on conditions; can use an abstraction when its use is given	• What are some examples of this concept? • In what way(s) can you classify these objects or ideas? • Based on what you know now, what do you think will happen next? • What instrument(s) can you use to find the mass of the object?
Application: use of theory, principles, ideas, or methods to solve a problem; use an abstraction correctly in a new situation	• What are some ways you can apply this concept or principle to your life? To your environment? • Can you design a product that uses this principle? • Can you explain why _____ happened?
Analysis: breaks down material into component parts; detection of relationships of the parts and of the way they are organized	• How are the criteria similar to and different from your sample? • How is _____ similar to or different from ____? • What is the cause/effect relationship here? • How would you describe the relationships between concepts shown on a diagram or graphic organizer? • How do the data you collected support your hypothesis? How do your data compare to others? What data are relevant to the problem? • What trends are shown on the graph?
Synthesis: putting together of elements from many sources and parts to form a whole; involves some uniqueness or originality in design of a new pattern or structure	• How would you teach this concept to another? • Can you create a useful model from these components? • Can you invent a new product? • What are some different ways you can test this hypothesis? • Can you analyze data and trends and design an action plan for learning more about a problem or issue or for solving a problem?
Evaluation: making of judgments about the value of ideas, works, solutions, methods, and so forth; using criteria and (internal or external) standards for appraising	• What criteria would you use to assess ____? • How will this plan help you to meet the standards we are trying to reach? • What methods were the most effective? • What score would you give this product or plan and why? • Why were some of the proposed solutions to the problem faulty?

Figure 3.6	The Five E's Model With Questioning Strategies	
Phase of Instruction	*Description of Phase*	*Questioning Strategies*
ENGAGE	• Capture student attention and promote wonder through experiences, stories, novelty, demonstrations, or other • Raise scientifically relevant questions • Create a context	• Ask students what they know and would like to know about a topic, concept, or issue • Identify misconceptions • Encourage students to ask operational questions around which investigation and research can be structured
EXPLORE	• Identify and describe action plan • Establish guidelines for guided or student-constructed inquiries or other worthwhile experiences • Describe the information or data students will collect and record • Emphasize importance of data to answer questions and support new learning	• Identify one or more inquiry questions as a focus for instruction; ask students how they would like to investigate questions • Ask questions related to procedures, use of equipment, data, calculations, insights, problems, and so forth, as they relate to instruction
EXPLAIN	• Allow students to reflect on process, thinking, data, and conclusions • Permit students to communicate and justify their explanations • Create meaning through reflection and discussion • Identify discrepancies and misconceptions	• Design a set of thought-provoking questions that allow students to explain what they did and what they learned • Ask questions that prompt students to formulate explanations from evidence and connect explanations to scientific knowledge • Use good questioning strategies such as "wait time" and show respect for student comments and questions
ELABORATE	• Make connections to personal lives, to technology, and to society • Link new learning to prior learning • Include opportunities to learn more or further clarify learning • Provide opportunities for relearning • Identify resources for extended learning	• Use questions to encourage and guide students to connect new learning to prior learning and apply learning • Identify new questions students have • Allow opportunities for relearning and extend learning
EVALUATE	• Use formative assessment strategies to provide evidence of learning throughout instruction and following instruction • Use evidence to determine concept understanding and skill development	• Ask questions that allow students to describe or show concept understanding • Ask questions that allow students to show evidence of thinking and skill development

Questions that might be asked during instruction include the following:

- Can you show me an example of . . . ?
- What did you think would happen?
- How or why did . . . happen?
- Can you provide evidence for this?
- Have you thought about . . . ?
- How are you controlling the variables?
- How was this piece of equipment useful to you?
- How are you making sure your measurements are accurate?
- Are your data consistent?
- Does this concept or phenomenon relate to a community problem or issue?
- How is your group helping one another to work through this project or process?
- What recommendations do you have for more effective learning?
- What new questions do you have?

Questions to Create Meaning

In the explanation and evaluation phases of the lesson, questions may be asked that require students to reflect on the inquiry question, the processes used to answer the question, the data that were generated or the information that was acquired, the conclusions that were drawn based on new data or information, and the applications to technology and society that created meaning.

The responses to the questions, along with products generated through instruction, such as models, data tables, graphs, and graphic organizers, enable teachers to determine how well students are progressing toward mastering specific objectives and help to identify possible misconceptions students may have developed.

Questions Aligned with Inquiries

Different types of inquiries require different types of questions for ongoing assessment of student learning. In Figure 3.7, four types of inquiries—investigations, decision-making or problem-solving tasks, technological design and inventions, and defense of a position—are identified along with a set of questions that might be asked to gain insight into student thinking and learning in each of these modalities.

Figure 3.7	Questions Related to Types of Inquiry
Types of Inquiry	*Questions*
Investigations	• What was your hypothesis? What evidence do you have to support it? • What process did you use? How did this help you? • What data did you collect? Were the data consistent? How did you organize your data? Did the data provide the evidence you needed to answer the inquiry question? • What types of technology, equipment, and resources did you use and how were they helpful? • What did you learn from this investigation? • How does the new learning link to your prior knowledge? • In what ways can you apply your learning to your life, to technology, or to society?
Decision-Making or Problem-Solving Tasks	• What was the problem or decision you needed to make? • What procedures did you use to get the data or information you needed? • How much and what types of data did you need to solve the problem or make the decision? • What materials and resources did you use? • What decision did you make? Can you support it with data? • What is one solution to the problem? Is there more than one? • What are the trade-offs, if any, to the solution?
Technological Design and Inventions	• What was your invention designed to do? Was your design successful? • How will your invention be an improvement over others like it? • What scientific principles did you apply? • How did you construct your model? Were some materials better than others for this product? Would you be able to create a similar product from different materials? • What resources provided information for this project? • What did you learn from this experience that will help you better understand technology and technological design?
Defend a Position	• How did this issue or problem affect you emotionally? Economically? Personally? Why did you select it? • What are the conflicting beliefs related to this issue? What was your prior belief? • What is the difference between fact and opinion? What data will you need to collect and record? • What were some ways you acquired new data to support your position? • What new evidence or data did you find to support your position? • Have your ideas about the problem or issue changed? • What argument and data will you use to defend your position? • What questions still remain? How will you address those?

4

Notebooks, Reports, and Graphic Organizers

Students at all levels should be encouraged to ask inquiry questions that can be answered by investigating and problem solving. Written and visual displays of conceptual and procedural knowledge provide a wealth of information about student learning, which can inform and guide instruction. Notebooks, reports, and graphic organizers are powerful tools for providing insight into student thinking and ways of knowing.

NOTEBOOKS

What Are They?

Science notebooks are a means of recording many aspects of thinking and learning throughout a unit of instruction. Notebook entries are generally predetermined to align with instructional goals and investigations, but they may be constructed by students as they work through guided or open inquiries or problem-based learning.

Why Do We Use Them?

Science programs that emphasize the use of student notebooks have been found to increase the language proficiency test scores as well as science achievement test scores of participating students. Scores on state-mandated science tests also showed significant gains for students participating in inquiry science programs that used notebooks (Klentschy, Garrison, & Maia Amaral, 2000).

Notebooks enable students to focus attention on the content and the processes of science for an extended period of time. Through the use of notebooks, students keep records of their thoughts, actions, and learning as they progress through a unit of instruction. Notebooks provide an excellent way to integrate writing and critical thinking into the science curriculum.

What Do They Look Like?

Students act like working scientists when they keep detailed notes of their questions, ideas, investigations, and discoveries. Teacher or teacher-student designed notebook entries should align with instructional objectives and the activities and experiences that address them. Notebooks provide opportunities for students to record and communicate their thinking and learning through writing, drawing, and illustrating.

Like many tools for learning, notebooks will take different forms depending on their purpose and the nature of the instructional experience. Notebook entries might include action plans for investigations or experiments, including the inquiry questions, predictions, procedures, data tables and visuals, conclusions, and applications of learning. Notebooks may also be used to record questions, predictions, and findings related to field and school site investigations or projects, science-related writing assignments, career information or research, community involvement, or other educational experiences.

As an example, Figure 4.1 shows seven categories of notebook entries for an investigation and the types of information that might be recorded under each category. From this list, a task-specific rubric can be developed to guide instruction. Note that the entries address components of inquiry-based science and relate to instructional goals. Entries may also address goals in mathematics, literacy, and other areas of the curriculum.

■ NOTEBOOKS AS ASSESSMENT TOOLS

As a tool for formative assessment, notebooks provide a great deal of information about learning to inform instruction. For example, students are more likely to engage in group discussions based on what they did and what they learned if they have the support of their notebooks. Sharing data and conclusions through small group or class discussion may identify discrepancies or misunderstandings, pointing to a need for relearning or modification of instruction.

Teachers can make periodic checks of notebooks to assess accuracy of work, monitor a student's progress toward reaching goals, and inform instruction. Informal observations of notebook entries may be made throughout instruction through interaction with students' notebooks, which provide useful information for teacher-student interviews and parent conferences.

Figure 4.1 Notebook Entries and Descriptions for an Investigation

Categories of Notebook Entries	Descriptions of Entries
Inquiry Questions or Problem; Purpose of Investigation	• Tells what students know and want to know • Clearly written in student words • Relates to important concepts
Prediction	• Connects to prior experience or knowledge • Need not be correct but is plausible and thoughtful • Relates to questions • Offers explanation or reason for the prediction
Action Plan and/or Procedures for Investigation	• Reasonable and relates to question • Clear sequence of events and directions • States materials needed for the investigation • Identifies observations that will be made for investigations or variables that will be tested and controlled for an experiment • Data organizers designed and used appropriately
Observations and Data	• Relate to question and plan • Well organized and accurate • Shown in appropriate words, drawings, charts, graphs, and numbers • Graphics appropriately titled and labeled
Conclusion and Connections	• Identify the "aha" or insights supported by data • Clear statement of findings described in own words • Links to inquiry question, procedures, and data or other evidence • Reflective thought • Connections to personal life, technology, and society
Reflection and Meaning	• Describe learning in relation to the context • Relate to concepts, skills, and habits of mind • Link science to other areas of the curriculum • Show connections to personal lives, to technology, and to community, state, nation, or the global society • Show evidence of understanding of relevance of learning
Next Steps/ Formulating New Questions	• Include student-generated ideas and new questions that are worthy of research • Add extensions and applications of original inquiry question; may include reading, interview, Internet, or other research • May include an action plan for further study

■ RUBRIC FOR A SCIENCE NOTEBOOK

Figure 4.2 shows a rubric for a science investigation that might be recorded in a notebook. The rubric includes performance levels for six categories of entries related to an investigation. Under each of the categories are bullet points that help to describe the category. A more accurate description of each category should be determined by the specific investigation. The rubric may include additional categories such as correct use of grammar and spelling, organizational skills, habits of mind, attention to detail, background information or research, use of technology, or others related to instructional goals.

A description for each of the four performance levels should be determined in advance by teachers and students so that students have a good understanding of the quality and quantity of work that is expected at each performance level. Students should be well aware of what is involved in meeting and exceeding the expectations.

When students are provided with a rubric or assist with the design of a rubric to guide their work, they are better able to take responsibility for their learning. With this tool, students are able to assess their work in an ongoing manner, recognize strengths and weaknesses, work toward higher standards, and develop confidence in their ability to produce higher quality work.

■ LAB REPORTS

What Are They?

Laboratory reports are written documentation of experiments and investigations in the professional world. Lab reports communicate the processes and results of work to management for decision-making purposes, and they archive work so that it will not have to be repeated in the future. The use of lab reports in the science classroom provides another way for instruction to resemble the work of scientists in the field.

Why Do We Use Them?

Unlike notebook entries that record student thinking and work throughout a unit of instruction, lab reports are used to summarize individual laboratory investigations or experiments. Lab reports provide a framework for students to show thinking and understanding of content and process as they work through an investigation and make sense of their findings.

What Do They Look Like?

Lab reports may follow a standard framework or be designed to align with specific investigations and experiments. Components of a report will vary depending on the nature of the task and the age and ability level of students. Six components are shown in Figure 4.3 with descriptions of what the component should include. In designing the report, teachers—with input from students—may wish to delete some requirements or add others to the categories to reflect instructional goals or personal preferences.

| Figure 4.2 | Rubric for Science Notebook |

Topic: _____

Categories of Entries for a Science Investigation	Exceeds	Meets	Lacking	Missing	Comments
Inquiry Question • Relevant • Clear/concise • Worthy of study					
Prediction • Draws from prior knowledge • Relates to inquiry question • Is logical and reasonable					
Investigation • Includes a clear action plan • Follows a logical sequence of steps using process skills • Identifies variables (if appropriate) • Describes data that will be generated or types of observations					
Observation and Data Collection • Correctly labeled data tables, graphs, and graphic organizers are used, as appropriate • Observations described in words or pictures • Data are accurate					
Processing and Thinking • Reflects on process, observations, and data • Conclusions relate to inquiry question and are supported by observations and data • Identifies discrepancies or problems (if appropriate) • Values integrated, meaningful learning					
Applications and Connections • Identifies connections to technology, personal life, community, or society • Creates and describes meaning • Identifies new questions for extended learning					

- *Title and Abstract:* The component of the report includes an appropriate title and an abstract describing the lab experience without specific detail. The abstract may state objectives, describe methods, summarize important results, and state major conclusions and their significance.

- *Introduction:* The introduction describes the problem and summarizes relevant research that provides a context and key concepts. The review of research may also provide a rationale for the research (inquiry) question.
    The introduction includes the steps that are being taken to answer the question and briefly describes the experiment by stating

    1. the research question

    2. the hypothesis

    3. the experimental design or methods for answering the question

- *Procedures:* The introduction is followed by the procedures. This heading has two subtitles: materials and methods. Under *materials*, the students describe what materials, subjects, and equipment were used, and under *methods*, they explain the steps used throughout the experiment.

- *Results and Conclusions:* This part of the report may begin with a sentence or two about the experiment followed by a summary of the most important findings. The results should be supported by data.
    Conclusions should describe the patterns, principles, or relationships the results show and include an explanation of how the results relate to the expectations and literature. Students should analyze their findings to determine if they agree, contradict, or show an exception to what was expected or found in the literature. The results of a study may lead to new questions and extended research.

- *Applications:* An additional component may be added to the report stating the implications of the study. Here the students may describe ways the study relates to their lives, to technology, and to community, state, national, or global problems or issues. They may make suggestions based on their findings or describe how the results of their experiment aid in their understanding of a broader topic.

- *Resources:* A list of books, articles, reports, Web sites, and other resources used should be included.

LAB REPORTS FOR ◼
LEARNING AND ASSESSMENT

Lab reports provide templates for guiding students through thoughtful and logical processes for asking testable questions, conducting experiments, and reporting the results of their work. Lab reports help students to understand the nature of science, the work that scientists do, and the importance of research for acquiring knowledge and formulating theories.

As an assessment tool, they provide a way for teachers and students to assess many aspects of learning that relate not only to science, but to other areas of the curriculum. Figure 4.3 shows a template based on the six components described previously.

Figure 4.3 Template for a Science Lab Report

Name: _____   Date: _____

Title of Investigation: _____

Abstract
Objectives
Methods
Summary of results
Major conclusions and significance

Introduction
Description of the problem
Summary of relevant research
Rationale for research question
Brief explanation of question, hypothesis,
   and experimental design or methods

Procedures
Materials
Processes and methods—explanation
   of steps used throughout the experiment

Results and Conclusions
Summary of findings
Data support
Explanation of how results relate to expectations

Applications
Implications of the study
Connections to personal lives, technology, or society
Suggestions or insights are shared (optional)

Resources

■ RUBRIC FOR A LAB REPORT

While the framework for the lab report provides a useful guide for the work, a rubric will help students to better understand the expectations for each of the components and enable them to assess the quality of their work.

The rubric in Figure 4.4 includes the categories of the lab report described in Figure 4.3. The rubric is analytic inasmuch as the parts of the report are scored separately. Most of the components include several indicators of learning that must be considered when scoring the report.

Four performance levels are shown, and those that meet or exceed expectations are based on quality of work rather than on quantity. Both quality and quantity of work are considerations for those reports that do not meet expectations, and indicators that are inadequate or missing can be circled on the rubric. There will be some subjectivity in determining whether work exceeds expectations or merely meets expectations. Samples of exemplary work and a discussion of the differences between the four performance levels will help students understand the expectations.

On the sample rubric, numbers are included for each performance level, which, when added, produce an overall score for the report. The score is not a grade but, rather, an indication of the quality, quantity, and accuracy of the report. Students who do not meet the minimal standard of 12 points should be allowed to redo the investigation or continue to work on the report to meet the standards.

Figure 4.4   Rubric for a Lab Report

Part of Report	Exceeds Expectations 3	Meets Expectations 2	Does Not Meet Expectations 1	Not Present 0
Title and Abstract	Title is appropriate and informative Abstract includes: • a clear and concise overview of objectives and methods • a well-described summary of results and major conclusions • accurate and detailed statement of significance of study	Title is appropriate Abstract includes: • an overview of objectives and methods • a summary of results and major conclusions • statement of significance of study	Title is inappropriate and/or abstract is lacking in quality in one or more areas: • overview of objectives or method • summary of results and conclusions • statement of significance	Title and/or abstract missing

Part of Report	Exceeds Expectations 3	Meets Expectations 2	Does Not Meet Expectations 1	Not Present 0
Introduction	Describes the problem and links it to relevant research Gives a rationale for inquiry question Provides a brief but clear explanation of question, hypothesis, and methods	Describes the problem Summarizes relevant research Gives a rationale for inquiry question Provides an explanation of question, hypothesis, and methods	One (or more) is inadequate: • statement of the problem • relevant research • rationale for question • explanation of question, hypothesis, and methods	One or more components missing
Procedures	Materials and equipment listed Includes a clear and detailed description of processes and methods used to investigate	Materials and equipment listed Includes a description of processes and methods used to investigate	Materials listed Description of processes and methods not clear or lacking in detail	Materials or description missing
Results and Conclusions	Includes a well-described summary of findings Findings are reasonable and well supported by data Includes a clear explanation of the relationship between results and expectations	Includes a summary of findings Findings are reasonable and supported by data Includes an explanation of the relationship between results and expectations	One (or more) is inadequate: • summary of findings • findings • data support • explanation of relationship between results and expectations	One or more are missing: summary, findings, supportive data, or explanation of relationship between results and expectations
Applications	Implications for the study are clearly described and meaningful Several connections are shown to personal life, technology, or society Suggestions or insights are described	Implications of study are described and meaningful A connection is made to personal life, technology, or society	Implications of study or connections to personal life, technology, or society are weak or lacking	Tables and graphs are lacking or inaccurate and without labels Observations, measurements, and calculations are inaccurate or missing
Resources	Resources exceed minimum, are varied and relevant to topic, and are presented in proper format	Adequate resources are relevant to topic and presented in proper format	Resources are lacking in number or not relevant to topic or are presented in improper format	Resources missing

■ GRAPHIC ORGANIZERS

What Are They?

Graphic organizers are visuals that enable students to show the ways they frame thought and knowledge. They show such things as descriptions of "big ideas," relationships between concepts, cause-and-effect relationships, links between new learning and prior learning, and applications of concepts.

Why Do We Use Them?

Research prepared by the Institute for the Advancement of Research in Education identified 29 scientifically based research studies that support the use of graphic organizers for improving student learning and performance across grade levels with diverse students in a broad range of content areas (Inspiration Software, Inc., 2003). Graphic organizers are powerful tools for creating mental models that aid the learner in retaining and recalling information. As a tool for formative assessment, they provide another means of capturing information about student thinking and learning.

What Do They Look Like?

There are at least six ways of organizing knowledge to show the relationships between concepts or between concepts and events. There is a variety of structures that can be used to display each of the types of relationships. What is more important than the visual is the underlying understanding of the relationships that it portrays.

Six types of relationships that can be shown on graphic organizers are described. Each of the six types has one or more organizational schemes. Figures 4.5–4.10 show one example of each type of relationship in the context of K–8 science with a brief explanation of each.

DESCRIPTIVE ORGANIZERS ■

Descriptive organizers enable students to view important ideas or concepts at the center along with subcategories or descriptive properties radiating from them. Sometimes linking words are included between boxes on the graphic to show relationships between the ideas or concepts.

Figure 4.5 shows the title for a unit of instruction and identifies the important concepts that will be addressed in the unit.

Figure 4.5   Concepts for a Unit on Properties of Water

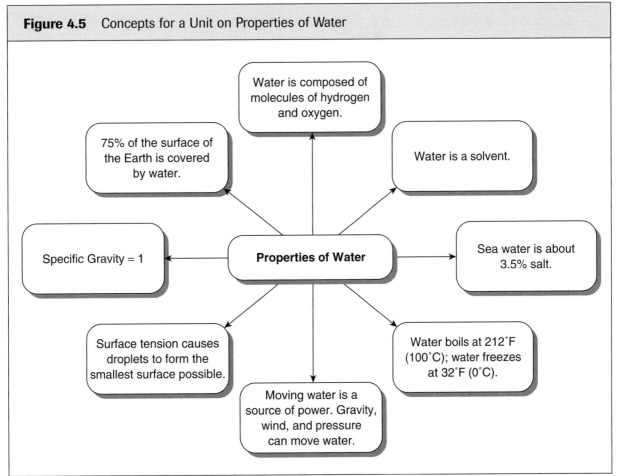

■ SEQUENTIAL ORGANIZERS

Sequential organizers show a series of events or ideas. These may take the form of a simple or elaborate flowchart or an historical timeline. Timelines, such as the one shown in Figure 4.6, are excellent ways for students to recognize the advancements in science throughout history and changes in technology over time.

Figure 4.6   Significant Events in the History of Space Exploration

1981	1983	1986	1988	1994
First U.S. space shuttle launched; John Young and Robert Crippen	Dr. Sally Ride: first woman in space; mission specialist on STS-7, launched from Kennedy Space Center, Florida, on June 18, 1983.	*Challenge* explosion kills seven astronauts and one teacher	*Discover* becomes first shuttle launched after *Challenger* accident	Scientists find black hole using Hubble Telescope

■ PROCESS-CAUSAL ORGANIZERS

Process-causal organizers identify stages in a process to show cause-and-effect relationships. The visual displays the "connectedness" of natural and human-created events. Often life cycles of insects or other animals are shown in this way. In physical science, multiple causes can lead to significant effects, as shown in the example in Figure 4.7.

Figure 4.7   The Ingredients for a Hurricane

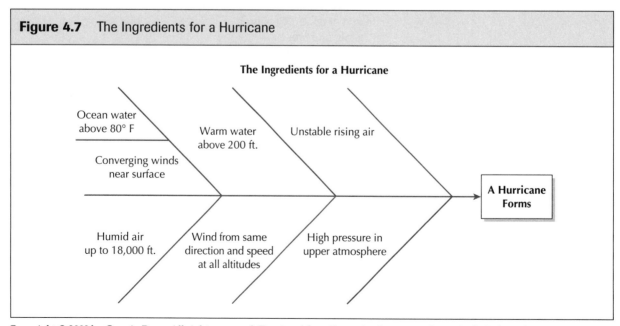

CATEGORICAL ORGANIZERS   ■

Categorical organizers show a hierarchy of ideas or concepts. "Big ideas" are shown with subtopics in horizontal or vertical tree-like configurations. This structure is often used to show the classification of living and nonliving things and may describe differences in the categories.

Figure 4.8 shows a simple classification system for tree leaves that describes differences between simple and compound leaves and shows examples of trees that have each type of leaf.

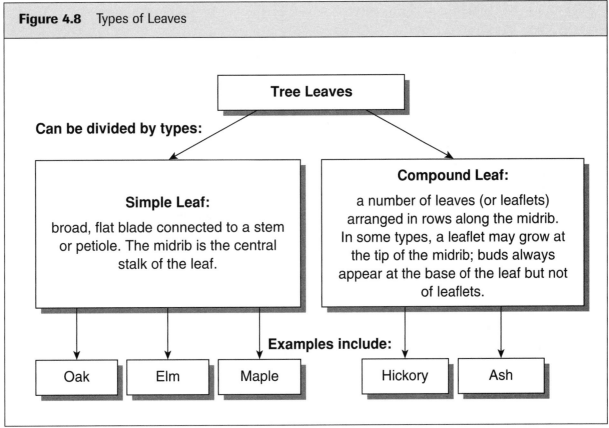

Figure 4.8   Types of Leaves

■ COMPARISON-RELATIONAL ORGANIZERS

Comparison-relational organizers provide a way to display similarities and differences between living and nonliving things or events. Students often identify the ways things are alike and the ways they are different, and the organizer enables them to visualize them. The Venn diagram shown in Figure 4.9 is often used for this purpose.

Figure 4.9   A Comparison of Plant and Animal Cells

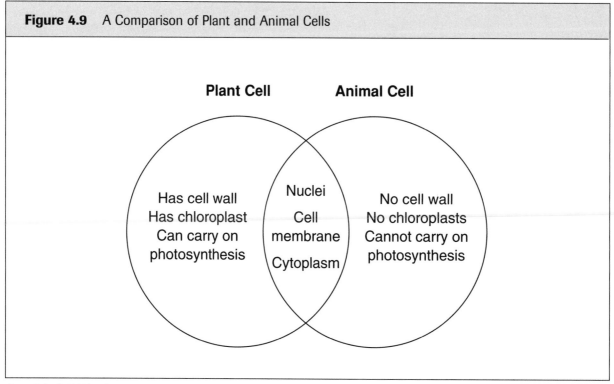

PROBLEM-SOLUTION ORGANIZERS   ■

Problem-solution organizers capture student thinking or findings related to solving a problem by showing plausible or identified solutions to the problem. For example, often students investigate an environmental problem or issue and propose solutions. Their findings can be summarized and shown on a graphic organizer similar to the one in Figure 4.10.

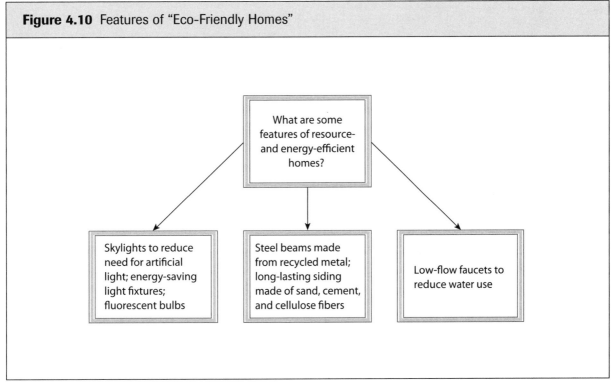

Figure 4.10 Features of "Eco-Friendly Homes"

■ FOUR-CORNER ORGANIZERS

Four-corner organizers are a type of descriptive organizer that provide space for recording information about four different, but related organisms, objects, or events. The visual enables students to make comparisons and identify similarities and differences. Figure 4.11 shows a four-corner organizer for comparing life cycles of animals.

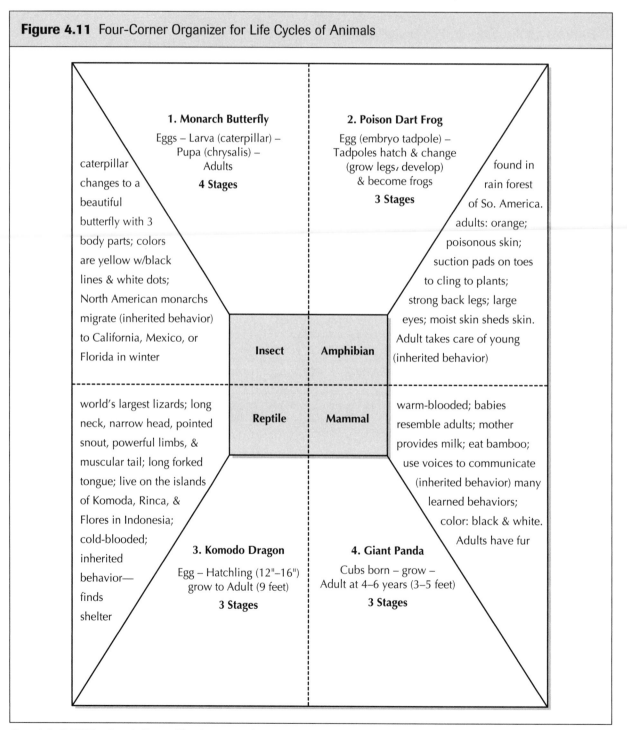

Figure 4.11 Four-Corner Organizer for Life Cycles of Animals

5

Projects and Presentations

LEARNING THROUGH PROJECTS ■

What Are They?

Projects are in-depth studies of particular concepts, processes, or applications. Projects relate to a particular subject area and have a specific focus. They are rich with opportunities for engaging learners and for developing deep understanding at a variety of levels of readiness or interest. When well supervised and documented, projects can serve as both learning opportunities and assessments of learning.

Through projects, students are able to explore concepts as investigators and researchers and create new or novel products through which they demonstrate and describe understanding. Students often give presentations to share their learning. Projects that address important goals and standards may follow a set of predescribed guidelines, or they may be designed by students.

Why Do We Use Them?

Projects offer students opportunities to be involved in active learning through activities and experiences at the school, at home, or within the community. Projects are valuable learning experiences because they build on students' interests and satisfy curiosity.

Involving students in decision-making and providing them with choices have been shown to improve academic performance, enhance self-esteem, and develop higher-level reasoning skills (Kohn, 1999). Projects provide opportunities for students to make choices, develop self-directed learning skills, and work at complex and abstract levels that match their abilities.

Personally designed projects are highly motivating and allow for in-depth work on topics of interest to students in ways they learn best. Students may design projects to answer their questions about a topic, problem, or issue and include experiences of particular interest, such as a visit to a museum, zoo, crime lab, hospital, exploratorium, or technology center.

What Do They Look Like?

Projects often involve the development of new products such as models, sculptures, collages, dioramas, inventions, blueprints or illustrations, maps, news reports, puppet shows, posters, brochures, songs, audio and video tapes, or PowerPoint presentations. They may include investigations, experiments, interviews, site visits, internships, research, or other experiences that enhance learning.

■ ASSESSING PROJECTS

Projects can be assigned, chosen by students from a list or choice board, or designed by students. In order for the projects to be worthy of time and energy, they must be designed to address instructional goals and standards. Projects should be designed that immerse students in learning experiences that deepen their understanding of standards-related concepts; the history and nature of science; the relationships between science, technology, and society; and other aspects of scientific literacy.

A rubric can be designed that addresses the important components of the project. For instructional purposes, the rubric should focus on goal-related indicators of learning. Non–goal-related factors, such as name on the project, project title, number of pages, artistic quality of visuals, and so forth, should be dealt with separately. A well-designed rubric can be used by students to guide the development of their projects and serve as a tool for peer review and self-assessment.

A creative assessment is shown for assessing an understanding of simple machines. The rubric in Figure 5.1 assesses learning goals through the design and development of a brochure. The indicators of learning for the project are clustered under headings that relate to the science education standards. Students should help to describe the quality of work expected for each of the performance levels.

ASSESSMENT FOR SIMPLE MACHINES AND INVENTIONS

Following the study of simple machines, students were given the guidelines for the design and development of a brochure that would demonstrate their understanding that complex machines are made up of simple machines and that technology has evolved and changed over time.

Content Category: Force and Motion— Simple Machines and Inventions

Level: Middle School

OVERVIEW: After studying simple machines, students will design and develop a brochure that shows and describes a compound technological innovation (invention) prior to 1930 (compound machine) and the simple machines that are part of the invention.

OBJECTIVES: Through the project students will:

- access information from a variety of sources
- provide a bibliography of resources
- identify the simple machines that make up the compound machine/invention
- identify and tell about the inventor to show that science is a human endeavor
- explain the historical development and change of an invention over time
- describe the connections between science, technology, and society for this invention
- synthesize information to fit the format of the brochure
- communicate ideas through illustration and show creativity
- demonstrate honesty and persistence throughout the project
- demonstrate motivation and self-direction

GUIDELINES: Create a three-fold brochure on 8.5 × 11–inch cardstock that shows and describes information about an invention prior to 1930 made up of simple machines. The brochure should include the following information.

1. The name of the invention and its inventor/creator
2. Biographical information about the inventor and a drawing of the inventor
3. Selection of an invention that is a complex machine made up of more than one simple machine and a detailed drawing of the invention with all of the simple machines labeled
4. Information about the invention, including what it was designed to do and why it was an innovation for its time
5. A brief explanation of how it has changed over time and how it looks today
6. A bibliography of resources used—at least two different types

■ RUBRIC FOR A PROJECT

A rubric should be developed that shows the indicators of learning that will be expected on the project. Note that the rubric identifies the science standards that are addressed. A rubric for the brochure project is given in Figure 5.1.

Figure 5.1 Rubric for the Brochure Project

Indicators of Student Learning	Exceeds Expectations	Meets Expectations	Does Not Meet Expectations	Comments
Concept Understanding				
Shows an appropriate invention and identifies the component simple machines accurately				
Describes the invention and explains why it was an innovation for its time				
History of Science				
Provides name, picture, and biographical information of the inventor				
Provides information about the machine/invention, including what it was designed to do				
Relationship Between Science-Technology-Society				
Describes how the invention has changed over time and how it looks today				
Communication Skills				
Accesses and uses information from a variety of sources and provides a bibliography or resources				
Analyzes, organizes, and synthesizes information to fit a format				
Communicates ideas through illustration				

Indicators of Student Learning	Exceeds Expectations	Meets Expectations	Does Not Meet Expectations	Comments
Dispositions				
Demonstrates honesty and persistence				
Demonstrates motivation and self-direction				

LEARNING THROUGH PRESENTATIONS ■

What Are They?

Presentations often accompany projects and include a variety of ways that students can communicate their learning to others. Presentations may be oral or visual. Through presentations, students are able to share their ideas, inquiry questions, strategies, information, conclusions, and new understandings in unique and exciting ways.

Why Do We Use Them?

Presentations allow students to communicate important aspects of their work and their learning and help them refine their communication skills. Presentations require students to organize information and plan and deliver it in logical and meaningful ways.

Presentations allow the audience to view the project from the student's perspective, and as an assessment tool, they enable a viewer to determine the depth and accuracy of the work that is presented. A rubric may be used to assist students in the design and delivery of the presentation.

What Do They Look Like?

Students may design and deliver presentations with a group or individually. Effective presentations include the use of visuals such as models, pictures, posters, or media such as PowerPoint or other slide shows. A presentation may include a demonstration or include role-play using project-related props, or it may engage the audience in an activity.

ASSESSING PRESENTATIONS ■

The rubric for a presentation should identify important content and skill-related goals and may include goals for effective communication. Figure 5.2 shows a rubric for the presentation of a project. In this example, the analytic rubric has only two performance levels for each indicator of learning. The indicator is described, and the student's performance either meets the expectation or does not meet it. Students should be well aware of what is expected for each of the indicators of learning.

There is space on the rubric for the assessor to record comments that identify strengths and weaknesses and to make suggestions for improvement. With useful feedback, students can focus on ways to improve their presentations in the future. The rubric may be used for peer assessment. Students will focus more closely on the important components of presentations if they are responsible for recording information.

Figure 5.2   Rubric for a Presentation

Indicators of Student Learning	Meets Expectations	Needs Improvement	Comments
Provides a clear overview of project and goals			
Describes a variety of strategies and resources to communicate ideas			
Organizes content effectively and shows understanding of concepts			
Is able to answer questions related to learning and connections			
Uses technology or other resources appropriately and effectively			
Shows evidence of critical thinking			
Captures and maintains attention of audience			
Demonstrates effective presentation skills (organization of content, eye contact, clear speech, time, etc.)			

6

Performance Tasks and Embedded Assessments

PERFORMANCE ASSESSMENT ■

What Is It?

One can argue that any assessment that requires activity on the part of students is performance assessment. However, performance assessment is generally defined as a single task or set of tasks that involves students actively and requires them to display their understanding of concepts and skills in words, pictures, products, or actions.

Performance assessments are two-dimensional because, by nature, they are used to both teach and assess. They engage students in content-rich investigations or challenging problem-solving tasks through which they demonstrate conceptual and procedural knowledge. Performance assessment should be anchored in tasks that reflect the ways that professionals operate and are challenged in the field and provide useful information to guide or modify instruction to better meet students' learning needs.

Why Do We Use Them?

Performance assessments have the same qualities and characteristics that are evident in good instruction—they engage students and challenge them to actively accomplish complex and significant tasks. In addition, performance assessments

- encourage teachers to develop assessments that match important goals and standards
- are rooted in interesting and meaningful contexts
- assess a broad range of indicators of learning by providing opportunities for students to show concept understanding and use of skills from more than one discipline
- enable students to demonstrate high levels of thinking and problem solving
- provide a means for monitoring student growth and learning over time in important categories of learning

Performance assessments engage students in worthwhile experiences that build and show concept understanding, develop and demonstrate skills and dispositions, and relate science to personal lives, technology, and the global community. Integrated performance assessments demonstrate the interdisciplinary nature of science and offer opportunities to assess not only learning in science, but learning in mathematics, literacy, and other areas of the curriculum as well.

What Do They Look Like?

Performance tasks should be an essential part of instruction. They may take the form of activities, investigations, presentations, or demonstrations of learning and be challenging, interesting, and engaging. Tasks should deepen students' understandings of concepts and skills while providing information about what they know and are able to do.

Two types of performance tasks will be described in this chapter: simple problem-based performance tasks using a paper/pencil or hands-on format that assess a single concept or skill, and multistage performance assessments that focus on a problem or issue, include one or more inquiry-based activities, and assess a broad range of concepts and skills. This type of performance assessment is useful for benchmark assessment.

■ PERFORMANCE TASKS

Single-focus performance tasks are a quick and easy way to gather information about student learning. They require students to demonstrate their thinking, concept understandings, and skills in a nonthreatening way. This type of assessment often follows teacher- or student-directed instruction and may take the form of a paper/pencil task, demonstration of a skill, or a notebook entry. Performance tasks are especially useful for assessing learning that may be difficult to measure as it is happening, as in the case of long-term investigations, projects, or contract learning.

Figures 6.1 and 6.2 show a number of performance tasks at the primary, intermediate, and middle grade levels. Note that the examples are thoughtfully linked to objectives related to major content areas of science found in national and state standards projects.

Figure 6.1 Performance Tasks for the Primary and Intermediate Grades	
Content Area	*Performance Tasks*
Properties of Objects	Task 1: Sort the objects on the table into two groups using one property. Write the name of the property you used and tell why you sorted the objects the way you did. Separate the objects using another property. Write the name of the new property. Task 2: Use the two magnets to demonstrate your understanding of "attract" and "repel." Task 3: List or tell four properties of the stuffed animal you are using (color, shape, size, or features). List or tell two ways that you and the stuffed animal are alike and two ways you are not alike. Estimate how many "animals" tall you are. Show or tell how you arrived at your estimate.
Characteristics of Organisms	Task 1: Draw a picture of a pet or other animal. In your picture, draw and label at least three things that the animal needs for survival. Explain your drawing. Task 2: Make a drawing or a collage (using magazine pictures) of the human body part that is associated with each of the five senses. Next to each sense organ, write one or more examples of the type of information we get from that sense.
Life Cycles of Organisms	Task: Draw and label the stages in the life cycle of a dog or cat (or chick, meal worm, cricket, butterfly, or other animal that was studied or that is similar to one that was studied). Write or describe two observable characteristics of the organism at each state. Use arrows to show the sequence of changes that occurs throughout the life cycle. Write a sentence or two to explain the life cycle.
Organisms and Their Environments	Task: Draw a picture of a park or other natural area. Draw a simple food chain that might be found in the environment. Label each part of the food chain. Be sure to include the source of energy for the food chain. Tell what would happen to the other members if one member of your food chain were no longer available.
Changes in Earth and Sky	Task 1: Draw a picture of a thermometer, a weather vane, and a rain gauge. Next to each picture tell what each of the instruments is used for. Write or tell how weather changes throughout the year. Another option: Demonstrate the use of one or more of the instruments for determining conditions of weather: a thermometer, a weather vane, and a rain gauge. Task 2: Draw the stages of change in the moon over the course of a month. Label the stages. Be prepared to describe (or write about) why the changes take place.

PERFORMANCE TASK K–4: CHANGES IN EARTH AND SKY

CONTEXT: Students have been studying weather. They observed that the weather changes from day to day and over seasons. They discussed the changes in plants and natural phenomena throughout a year, how clothing and other personal needs change from season to season, and the ways their outdoor activities are affected by weather.

Students used thermometers to read and record outdoor and indoor temperatures, a weather vane to observe and record wind direction, and a rain gauge to measure and record precipitation.

ASSESSMENT: Through this assessment task, students will demonstrate an understanding of instruments that are used to record weather. They will describe weather patterns and changes in their geographic area throughout a year and demonstrate their understanding that weather affects the decisions they make about how to dress and what they do outdoors.

TASK: Draw a picture of a thermometer, a weather vane, and a rain gauge. Next to each picture write or tell how each instrument helps us understand the weather.

Write or tell how weather changes throughout the year where you live. Write or tell two ways that weather affects your area, the decisions you make, and your outdoor activities.

PERFORMANCE TASK 5–8:
TRANSFER OF ENERGY IN A FOOD CHAIN

CONTEXT: Students have learned that the source of energy for photosynthesis comes from sunlight and that sunlight is necessary for green plants to grow. Plant-eating animals (herbivores) are first-order consumers while animals that feed on other animals (carnivores) are secondary consumers. Some animals (omnivores) eat both plants and animals. Students should be able to explain the transfer of energy from one level to the next and that populations of organisms lower on the food chain need to be much greater to support those higher on the food chain.

ASSESSMENT: Through this task students will show an understanding of the transfer of energy within a system and that the loss of an important component of a system produces a state of disequilibrium that affects the entire system.

TASK: Draw a picture or a diagram to show a food chain that includes the source of energy, producers, and a primary consumer. Label each part.

Explain how the food chain shows a transfer of energy.

Write what would happen if one of the components of the food chain you drew were to disappear from the ecosystem due to loss of habitat, loss of food source, natural disasters such as fire, flood, or volcanic action, or human intervention

Figure 6.2   Performance Tasks for Upper Intermediate and Middle Grades

Content Area	Performance Task
Properties and Changes of Properties in Matter	Task: Consider the objects on the table. Use the balance and mass set, the graduated cylinder, beakers, water, and any other materials in the classroom to serial order the objects by density. Draw the objects from the most dense to the least dense.
Transfer of Energy	Task 1: Make a drawing to illustrate the principle: Heat moves in predictable ways, flowing from warmer objects to cooler ones, until both reach the same temperature. Label the drawing and be prepared to explain it.

Task 2: Draw a picture or a diagram to show a food chain that includes the source of energy, producers, and a primary consumer. Label each part. Explain how the food chain shows a transfer of energy. Write what would happen if one of the components of the food chain you drew were to disappear from the ecosystem. |
| Structure and Function in Living Systems | Task 1: Make a poster to show the levels of organization of living things, beginning with cells and ending with ecosystems. Be prepared to describe similarities and differences in the levels.

Task 2: Draw a cell and identify the organelles. Write the function of each organelle next to its name.

Task 3: Draw one of the systems of the human body. Label the organs and describe the function of each on the drawing. |
| Reproduction and Heredity | Task: Make a drawing to show the processes of meiosis and mitosis. Label the stages in the processes. Be prepared to explain the similarities and differences between the two processes. |
| Structure of the Earth System | Task 1: Draw a large boulder and show what will happen to it over time if it is acted upon by forces of weathering and erosion. Be sure to include a written description of the forces and the changes that occur.

Task 2: Choose one of the following contexts and explain how topographic maps could be useful: designing of a golf course, planning a hike through the mountains, building a road from mountains to the seashore. Include a visual as part of your explanation.

Task 3: Porosity versus grain size: Design and conduct an investigation to answer the question—Is the porosity of gravel, rocky sand, sand, and clay a function of grain size? Apply your findings to predict the amount of water that an aquifer of gravel might hold compared to the same size aquifer of sand. |
| Earth in the Solar System | Task: Draw a model of the solar system showing major and minor heavenly bodies. Describe their relationships to one another. Describe two forces acting on the solar system. |

■ A GENERALIZED RUBRIC FOR A PERFORMANCE TASK

Performance tasks may assess understanding of a single concept or multiple concepts. They may include dimensions of inquiry as well as understanding of concepts. Tasks generally include drawings as well as written or verbal explanations. A generalized rubric for a performance task is shown in Figure 6.3. The rubric should be modified to fit each specific performance task

Figure 6.3   A Generalized Rubric for Performance Tasks in Science

Indicators of Learning	Exceeds Standards	Meets Standards	Approaching Standards	Does Not Meet Standards
Understanding of Concepts/Principles				
Use of Terminology	• uses all available terminology • all used appropriately in explanation	• uses most available terminology • all or most used appropriately in explanations	• some use of terminology • some used inappropriately in explanations	• little/no use of appropriate terminology • terminology not used to describe or explain
Conceptual Knowledge	• accurate/clear explanations of concepts • deep understanding	• accurate/clear explanations of concepts • good understanding	• explanation vague or lacking in detail • little understanding	• explanation faulty or inappropriate • no understanding
Representation	• excellent use of graphic organizer(s) to show data and/or thought patterns • all used and labeled appropriately	• good use of graphic organizer(s) to show data and/or thought patterns • all or most used and labeled appropriately	• some attempt to use graphic organizer to show data and/or thought • some errors	• little/no use of graphic organizer(s) to organize data and/or show thought patterns • inappropriate use of graphic organizer(s)

Indicators of Learning	Exceeds Standards	Meets Standards	Approaching Standards	Does Not Meet Standards
Dimensions of Inquiry				
Use of Skills and Strategies (includes ability to understand and do inquiry, to apply skills and strategies)	• good understanding of inquiry • shows excellent and appropriate use of all skills and strategies	• shows understanding of inquiry • shows good and appropriate use of skills and strategies	• use of inquiry • shows minimal use of skills and strategies • some are used appropriately	• little or no use of inquiry • shows little or no use or inappropriate use of skills and strategies
Use of Tools and Technologies (rulers, balances, magnifiers and microscopes, A/V, models, and so forth)	• shows excellent and appropriate use of tools and technologies	• most used appropriately • shows good use of tools and technologies • all/most used appropriately	• shows some use of tools and technologies	• shows no/ little or inappropriate use of tools or technologies
Connections to Technology or Society	• excellent connections (with elaboration) to technology and society	• appropriate connections to technology or society	• weak connections to technology or society	• little/no connections to technology or society

EMBEDDED ASSESSMENTS ▪

Embedding assessment throughout instruction is the best example of formative assessment. In this case, instruction and assessment are intertwined and take the form of one or a series of activities with multiple opportunities to assess learning as it occurs. The information gained through this approach allows the assessor to provide immediate feedback to students about their learning, monitor student progress in meeting instructional goals, and modify instruction to meet student needs.

Embedding assessment in instruction requires thoughtful planning but rewards the assessor with an abundance of information about student learning from which to make decisions. Embedded assessments are powerful tools for diagnosing student strengths and weaknesses and helping students progress toward mastery of important goals and standards. The tools for formative assessment are shown in Figure 6.4. The trick is to integrate the strategies throughout instruction so that they provide feedback and enhance learning.

Figure 6.4 Tools for Formative Assessment
Observation checklists
Interviews, dialogue, and informal questioning
Science notebooks and lab reports
Products, projects, and presentations
Performance tasks
Criterion-referenced tests and writing prompts

Multidimensional performance tasks should reflect challenges that face professionals in the field. They may be "ill-structured," which means that there is more than one correct pathway to a solution. Students are actively involved in one or more of these ways:

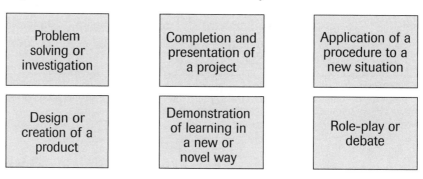

Interesting contexts can be developed that engage students in activities or investigations with opportunities for them to write, draw, demonstrate, and describe their learning. Such multidimensional tasks generally include

- the design and application of an action plan for investigating a question or solving a problem related to important content
- a sequence of activities that apply the skills of inquiry
- verbal or written explanations of concepts
- use of data tables, graphs, and graphic organizers
- open-ended questions for application and elaboration of concepts
- criterion-referenced quiz items to show understanding of major concepts, skills, or applications
- reading component with follow-up questions for comprehension
- writing component in the form of a prompt that relates to the context

A MODEL FOR EMBEDDED ASSESSMENT ■

A performance task based on a model offered by Hammerman and Musial (2008) includes a sequence of standards-based instructional activities with multiple tools for learning and assessing embedded throughout. The series of investigations dealing with the properties of magnetism are rooted in a student-friendly context. As students are engaged in activities, they are developing or reinforcing concepts, practicing skills, and developing and demonstrating habits of mind. While the activities focus on instruction, students are demonstrating mastery of conceptual and procedural knowledge. The variety of tasks included in the sample enables students to learn and to show learning in multiple ways.

The model includes a sequence of inquiry-based activities, sample criterion reference test items to assess basic concept understanding, and a writing prompt to assess the student's ability to apply learning to another situation.

Inquiry-Based Activities

Each of the inquiry-based activities that comprise the multidimensional task engages students in active learning using process and thinking skills that build concept understanding. Each activity includes the following information:

- title of activity
- description of the activity
- materials and safety
- suggestions for presentation and management
- student response sheets with appropriate data tables, graphs, charts, and space for drawings or explanations of conclusions or summaries of learning. Response sheets may also include questions for discussion, reflection, and application of learning.

Criterion-Referenced Test Items

Sample criterion-referenced multiple-choice items are included in the model. These can be developed and used to assess concepts at the knowledge and comprehension levels and provide another way for students to show understanding. There are three items that assess the same concept. If a student gets two or three of the items related to a particular concept correct, one might reasonably infer that the student understands the concept.

Writing Prompt

The writing prompt extends student thinking by asking them to apply their learning to a new situation. Responses to the writing prompt show concept understanding and the student's ability to apply the concepts of science to their lives or to technology or society.

Rubrics for the Performance Task

The analytic rubric provided for the performance task identifies indicators of learning in the order in which they occur in the activities and lists their standards-related unifying concept or process. The detailed rubric enables an assessor to monitor student concept understanding, skill application and accuracy, and applications of learning.

Indicators of learning related to writing and grammar that teachers may want to assess should be added to the rubric. It is important for teachers to remember that scientific literacy includes the skills of communication. Although habits of mind are not specifically identified in the rubric, the activities provide ample opportunities for students to demonstrate desirable behaviors such as perseverance, honesty, and the ability to work in a collaborative group. These may be assessed using an observation checklist.

■ SAMPLE EMBEDDED PERFORMANCE TASK

──────MAY THE FORCE BE WITH YOU──────

RATIONALE

This intermediate-level instructional sequence deepens student understanding of properties of matter and force using various types of magnets and materials. Students assume the role of scientists. Throughout the set of activities students make observations and inferences, collect data, draw conclusions, and apply their learning. They design a test to answer an inquiry investigation and investigate and discover the magnetic field.

The performance assumes that students are familiar with magnets and have done some preliminary work investigating magnetic properties of different objects. Students should know that metal objects are attracted to magnets, as opposed to plastic, glass, or wood.

- In Activity 1, students will learn that not all metal objects are magnetic and will make inferences about metal objects that exhibit magnetic properties.

- In Activity 2, students will be asked to design a test to determine how far objects can be from a magnet and still be attracted to it. This demonstrates their ability to measure and express an understanding of a magnetic field.

- In Activity 3, students will set up a test to determine what happens when the poles of magnets come together. This activity demonstrates their understanding of the effect magnets have on one another. The activity ends with an opportunity for students to apply their understanding of forces within a field.

Standards Alignment

National Science Education Standards (NRC, 1996)

- Objects can be described by the properties of the materials from which they are made, and those properties can be used to separate or sort a group of objects or materials. (p. 127)

- Magnets attract and repel each other and certain kinds of other materials. (p. 127)

*Project 2061 Statements From **Benchmarks for Science Literacy** (AAAS, 1993)*

- Without touching them, a magnet pulls on all things made of iron and either pushes or pulls on other magnets. (p. 94)

- People can often learn about things around them by just observing those things carefully, but sometimes they can learn more by doing something to the things and noting what happens. (p. 10)

Activity One: Metals That Attract

DESCRIPTION OF ACTIVITY

Students are given a variety of metallic objects and a magnet. They should test each object to determine if it is attracted to the magnet. Students will record data on the response sheet by using an X to show which objects are attracted and will explain their observations.

MATERIALS

- piece of aluminum foil
- penny
- nickel
- paper clip
- brass fastener
- safety or straight pin
- bottle cap
- bar, ring, or horseshoe magnets

PRESENTING THE ACTIVITY

In this activity, students will examine a variety of metallic objects to determine if they are attracted to a magnet. Instruct students to read the directions on the student response sheet and begin by making a prediction related to the inquiry question. They will then test the objects and record and describe their observations. Students will then make inferences based on their observations. For example, if students observe that not all metallic objects are magnetic, they might infer that only certain metals are attracted to magnets. Students should realize that findings, such as "not all metals are magnetic," lead scientists to new questions and investigations about the properties of materials.

The open-ended question included on the response sheet asks students to apply their understanding of the properties of magnets by suggesting how they might be useful to society. Such questions expand student thinking and address the relationships between science, technology, and society.

(Continued on page 81)

ACTIVITY ONE WORKSHEET   Name: _____

Date: _____

METALS THAT ATTRACT

Inquiry Question: Are all metal objects attracted to magnets?

I think _____

because _____.

You will be given a set of objects that are made of different types of metal. Test the objects to see if they are magnetic. Place an X next to the object(s) that are attracted by the magnet.

Object	Attracted? (X = yes)
Aluminum foil	_____
Penny	_____
Nickel	_____
Paper clip	_____
Brass fastener	_____
Pin	_____
Bottle cap	_____

Describe your observations:

_____
_____
_____

Based on your observations, what inference(s) can you make about the objects that are attracted to magnets?

_____
_____
_____
_____
_____

Think of an example of how a magnet might be helpful in accomplishing a task. Describe the task and explain how the magnet would help:

_____
_____
_____
_____
_____
_____
_____
_____
_____
_____

Activity Two: Close Encounters

DESCRIPTION OF ACTIVITY

In this task, students are asked to design an experiment to test whether objects must be in direct contact with a magnet to be affected by it. Students will make a prediction, describe a test or show one in a diagram, and perform the experiment. They are asked to design their own data tables and report the results. If students are not yet ready to design their own data tables, teachers may assist in developing an appropriate data table, or the class may decide on a single test and data table that all students will use.

Through careful observation, students will discover that objects do not have to be touching the source of the force (the magnet) acting on them in order for it to exert a push or pull.

MATERIALS

- Bar, ring, or horseshoe magnets
- Metal objects that are attracted to magnets from Activity 1
- Metric rulers or tape measure

PRESENTING THE ACTIVITY

This activity provides an opportunity for students to design and conduct their own tests and create their own data tables. However, if students are not ready to do this, a test and data table may be designed by the class through discussion.

Explain to students that they should follow the directions on the student response sheet and make a prediction with an explanation related to the inquiry question. They will conduct the test and collect and record data using the magnets and metal objects. Students will describe their conclusions based on the data they collect. Students may infer the presence of a magnetic field on their own. The question at the bottom of the response sheet implies the presence of a magnetic field and asks students to further infer what it may look like for the magnet they used.

Activity Three: Coming Attractions

DESCRIPTION OF ACTIVITY

In this activity, students will investigate what happens when the poles of two magnets come together in the following combinations: N-N, N-S, and S-S. Based on data, students should conclude that like poles repel while opposite poles attract.

The open-ended questions at the end of the activity ask students to think of magnetic attraction as a force and to view it as but one of many types of force that affect people in their everyday lives. Besides magnetic force, students may consider forces, such as gravitational, buoyant, electrical, and centripetal forces in their responses. They may also describe forces that are applied by humans.

MATERIALS

- two bar or ring magnets per person or team (if you are using ring magnets, put a red sticker on the N pates and a blue sticker on the S poles of the magnets)
- metric rulers or tape measures
- string
- scissors

Criterion-Referenced Test Items and Writing Prompt

Sample multiple-choice items are shown that address the standards-based concepts identified in the beginning of the performance. The items are written at the knowledge/comprehension levels since multiple-choice items lend themselves to that level of assessment. Conceptual knowledge at the application level is assessed through the various questions at the ends of the activities and through the writing prompt.

ANALYTIC RUBRIC

The detailed analytic rubric is offered as a prototype for the concepts and skills that might be assessed through the performance tasks. The rubric identifies the unifying concepts and processes of science from which the indicators of learning are generated and shows that the tasks also assess indicators of learning related to mathematics, literacy, and critical thinking.

A set of discrete indicators is identified for each of the activities and the writing prompt. They correspond to the order in which they are found in the tasks. Many of the indicators are followed by parentheses that either show the concept or skill category being assessed or provide additional clarification. This additional information is provided here to add clarification and to stress the importance of designing performances that both teach and assess concepts and skills related to goals and standards.

Three levels of performance are identified and a fourth column is offered for the addition of comments, suggestions, explanations, or other information that will provide feedback to students about their learning and guide them toward reaching the standards.

ACTIVITY TWO WORKSHEET

ACTIVITY TWO WORKSHEET

Name: _____

Date: _____

CLOSE ENCOUNTERS

Inquiry Question: How far can an object be from a magnet and still be attracted to it?

I think _____

because _____ .

Using the magnet and the metal objects, design a specific test that would answer the above question. Describe the test by writing or drawing it in the space provided.

Perform the test. Develop a data table to show your findings. Draw the table below. (If the distance you measure is less than 1 centimeter, use the symbol <. Example: For a measurement of 1/2 a centimeter, write < 1 cm to represent less than 1 cm on the table.

Write a conclusion:

_____

_____

_____

_____

_____

_____

_____

_____

Based on what you have observed, draw what the magnetic field might look like for the test you conducted.

ACTIVITY THREE WORKSHEET

Name: _____

Date: _____

COMING ATTRACTIONS

Inquiry Question: What happens when the poles of two magnets come together in the following combinations: N–N, N–S, S–S?

Identify the north and south poles of a bar magnet (or red/blue sides of a ring magnet).

Place the north pole (red side) of one magnet near the north pole (red side) of the other magnet. Record your observations below.

_____

_____

_____

_____

Place the north pole (red side) of the first magnet near the south pole (blue side) of the second magnet. Record your observations below.

_____

_____

_____

_____

Finally, place the south pole (blue side) of the first magnet near the south pole (blue side) of the second magnet. Record your observations below.

_____

_____

_____

_____

Summarize your findings.

Magnetic poles	Observations (attract = X; repel = 0)
North–North (red–red)	
North–South (red–blue)	
South–South (blue–blue)	

What conclusion can you draw about the behavior of the magnets?

_____

_____

_____

How is a magnet a type of force?

_____

_____

_____

List two examples of forces in the environment. Describe each force and tell how each affects people or objects. Demonstrate or draw pictures of the forces, if possible.

_____

_____

_____

_____

_____

_____

_____

_____

_____

_____

_____

_____

_____

CRITERION-REFERENCED TEST:
MAY THE FORCE BE WITH YOU

Answer the following multiple-choice questions related to the key concept of magnetic properties.

1. Which of the following objects will be attracted by a magnet?
   a. plastic cubes
   b. paper clips
   c. rubber bands
   d. paper strips

2. An object that pushes or pulls on another produces a
   a. force
   b. chemical
   c. change
   d. concept

3. A magnet produces a type of force because it
   a. has no effect on objects
   b. pulls on glass objects
   c. pushes or pulls on objects
   d. pushes on glass objects

4. When two magnetic poles are put close together, the result is
   a. gravitational pull
   b. no affect
   c. spinning of the magnets
   d. a push or pull

5. In order for a magnet to attract an object, it must be made of
   a. rubber
   b. plastic
   c. iron
   d. glass

6. Which diagram shows the correct way to put two bar magnets away so that the two ends will attract?

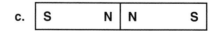

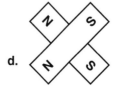

7. A magnet has a north pole and a south pole. Two bar magnets are hung by strings so that the two north poles are facing one another.

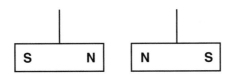

In this situation, the magnets will
a. push away from one another
b. pull toward one another
c. spin
d. have no effect on one another

8. When Mark put the south pole of one magnet near the north pole of another magnet, he found that they
a. pushed away
b. repelled
c. attracted
d. had no effect

9. Sally put a strong magnet on the table near a compass that shows direction. She observed that the needle on the compass moved. She inferred that the needle of the compass was made of
a. iron
b. plastic
c. glass
d. aluminum

WRITING PROMPT: A FRIEND IN NEED

Your cousin Terry is in charge of an aluminum recycling project. She has been given donations of all sorts of metal objects including some aluminum. She knows she has to separate the aluminum from the other metals but does not have an effective way to do this.

Since you had such an important role in helping design the first space robot that went to the moon, you have been asked to help your cousin design a robot to help sort the metal for the recycling project. Use what you have learned about magnets and metals in your design. Draw a picture of what the Metal Monster would look like. Of course, you will need an instruction manual to go along with the robot so that your cousin will know how to operate it. Keep the manual short—no more than two pages. It should include step-by-step instructions and may include pictures.

ANALYTIC RUBRIC: MAY THE FORCE BE WITH YOU

Indicators of Learning Relate to These Unifying Concepts and Processes

- Systems, Order, and Organization
- Evidence, Models, and Explanations
- Constancy, Change, and Measurement
- Evolution and Equilibrium
- Form and Function
- Mathematics, Literacy, and Thinking Skills

(Items in parentheses identify some of the concepts and skills assessed through the task.)

SCALE

	Complete	Almost	Not Yet	Comments
Activity 1: Metals That Attract **The student:** • Made a logical prediction and gave a reason • Recorded data for magnetic items (paper clip, brass fastener, pin) (Observation; Classification) • Observed that all metal objects are not magnetic (Observation; Explanation) • Inferred that all metal objects are not made of the same materials (student might know that some are made of iron and some of aluminum) • Gave an example of the usefulness of magnets (Concept Understanding and Application; S-T-S) • Explained how a magnet can be used to solve a problem (Problem Solving and Reasoning)				
Activity 2: Close Encounters **The student:** • Made a logical prediction and gave a reason • Described a test in words or drawings (Explanation; Representation; Communication) • Performed the test and showed a data table with reasonable measurements (Measurement; Reasoning) • Used symbols properly, if applicable • Wrote a logical conclusion to show concept understanding (Systems, Order, and Organization)				

(Continued)

(Continued)

	Complete	Almost	Not Yet	Comments
• Drew the magnet showing lines of force with limited range (possible magnetic field) (Form and Function; Models and Explanation)				
Activity 3: Coming Attractions **The student:** • Recorded observations for N-N • Recorded observations for N-S • Recorded observations for S-S (Observation; Record Data) • Summarized findings (Models and Explanation) • Drew a conclusion about the behavior of magnets (Evidence; Reasoning; Communication) • Described magnetic force (Concept Understanding; Explanation) • Identified two examples of forces in the environment (Concept Understanding and Application; S-T-S) • Described how forces affect people or objects (Concept Application)				
Criteria for A Friend in Need The instruction manual should: • Be organized with a sequence of logical steps • Include instructions that show an understanding of magnetic attraction (Form and Function) • (Optional) Include pictures that fit the sequence of steps and aid in understanding how to use the "robot" to help solve the problem (Concept Understanding and Application; S-T-S; Representation; Models and Explanation)				

Scoring Scale	
Complete	Student exhibited the indicator
Almost	Student showed some evidence that the indicator was exhibited, but something is incorrect or missing
Not Yet	Student did not show evidence of learning for that indicator

DESIGNING EMBEDDED ■
PERFORMANCE ASSESSMENTS

Hammerman and Musial (2008) identified ten steps for designing multidimensional performance tasks for learning and assessment. The steps are not necessarily sequential, but each is important to consider in the development of tasks that both teach and assess. Each step is identified and briefly described. What is most important is that the performances are authentic, meaning they are aligned with learning goals and represent ways that professionals are challenged in the field.

1. *Consider standards.*

   Review national, state, and local standards documents to identify the important goals that are relevant to the age and ability level of the students for whom the performance is being developed. For science, such a review might include *Science for All Americans* (AAAS, 1990), *Benchmarks for Science Literacy* (AAAS, 1993), and *National Science Education Standards* (NRC, 1996).

2. *Examine and discuss behaviors of scientists "in action."*

   Consider:

   • How do scientists use concepts and skills in the work they do?

   • What habits of mind do they exhibit in their work?

   • How do they communicate their work to others?

   Students can observe working scientists through videotape or televised programs, or visits to science labs, museums, zoos, and other informal learning centers. They may invite a scientist or engineer from the community to visit their classroom for an informal discussion of the work they do.

3. *Relate science at your grade level to components of "real-world" science.*

   Reflect on how science at your grade level compares to science in the professional world: (a) science concepts, (b) science process and thinking skills, (c) dispositions that working scientists display, and (d) applications and connections of concepts to technology and society.

4. *Design a meaningful context for what you want to assess.*

   Think about a context for assessing the important components of science and other areas of the curriculum that are identified as important. The context should involve students in a series of activities that relate to a problem or issue, involve making a decision or clarifying an issue, develop a point of view, or generate a project, product, or invention. Context may be designed around

   • student interests and questions

   • applications of science to problems, issues, and everyday actions within the community

- Gardner's multiple intelligences theory
- brain-based learning and emotional intelligence cultural diversity and issues

5. *Clarify and enrich the meaningful performance task.*

As you design the performance task, build in as many opportunities as possible for students to show what they know and can do. Create a rough draft of the performance task, then revisit the important concepts, skills, and habits of mind from science and other disciplines. Consider and add a variety of ways to gather information of student learning throughout instructional sequence.

6. *Identify the important elements of the performance task to assess.*

Consider what prior learning is required so that students are prepared for the performance task. Identify the concepts, process and thinking skills, and dispositions that can be taught or reinforced and assessed through the performance task. Include connections to mathematics, technology, and society whenever possible.

7. *Determine what an acceptable performance looks like.*

Teachers must identity important indicators of learning and clearly describe them in a rubric. This analytic approach will enable students to understand the nature and focus of the performance task.

8. *Establish a rubric for learning and assessment.*

For each of the indicators of learning, develop two or more levels of performance. Including students in a discussion of the indicators of learning and levels of mastery enables them to ask questions and clarify expectations.

9. *Communicating the performance task.*

It is important to write a complete and accurate description of the performance task for your own understanding and for other teachers who might wish to use the task.

10. *Field test the performance task and revise as needed.*

Once a performance task is developed, it should be tested with students to determine its effectiveness. Use the rubric to record data, provide feedback to students about their learning, and determine the effectiveness of the task. Allow students to use the rubric to self-assess, reflect on their learning, and evaluate the task for its intended purpose. Use student scores, comments, and reflections to clarify or revise the activities in the performance task and make necessary changes to the rubric.

PERFORMANCE ASSESSMENTS FOLLOWING INSTRUCTION   ■

Multiple and varied assessments used throughout instruction provide abundant data on which to make decisions. Although it is desirable to assess students throughout instruction, it is not always possible to collect the amount or type of data to inform decisions about student learning or to inform needed changes in instruction. A separate single-step or multi-step activity following instruction enables an assessor to observe student performance related to important learning goals and gather additional information needed to make informed decisions.

Assessments that follow instruction would be summative if their sole purpose were to identify what students know and are able to do and to assign a score or grade. The performances are formative if they are used to diagnose strengths and weaknesses in student learning and are followed by opportunities for relearning through tutoring, take-home or afterschool activities, classroom activity centers, projects, media presentations, or direct instruction.

SAMPLE PERFORMANCE ASSESSMENTS   ■

Two examples of performance assessment that follow instruction are shown here.

- The first example follows instruction dealing with the structure of plants and the functions of major plant parts and their usefulness to society.

- The second example has two parts.

    1. Part I describes student-conducted research on the characteristics of planets in the solar system.

    2. Part II assesses the student's understanding of adaptation and ability to apply characteristics to a fictitious creature that would be able to survive on a planet other than Earth.

PERFORMANCE ASSESSMENT #1
WHAT I KNOW ABOUT PLANTS

DESCRIPTION AND PURPOSE: This performance assessment was designed to follow instruction of important concepts in a unit on plants. Throughout instruction, observation checklists, notebook entries, lab work, interviews, and discussion were used to gather data about student learning.

This performance assessment provides an additional measure of what students know and are able to do.

KEY CONCEPTS: Standards-related concepts were the focus for a unit dealing with the structure and function of plants. The concepts around which the unit of instruction was designed are shown here.

(Continued)

(Continued)

- Four main parts of plants are the stem, leaves, root, and flowers, and each part has a specific structure and function that serves the plant and allows the plant to live, grow, and reproduce. Seeds are not all alike.

- Leaves can be classified in a variety of ways based on properties such as venation, shape, size, type, and description. Properties of leaves can be observed using a magnifier. A dichotomous key is a system of classification based on properties. Leaves can be classified into one of two categories based on whether they have or do not have a specific property.

- The age of trees or branches can be determined by studying the cross-sections. For each year of growth, the tree grows an additional layer of cells, which adds an annual ring.

- Plant cells can be observed firsthand by using a microscope. Plant cells have a nucleus, chloroplasts, a cell wall, cytoplasm, and a cell membrane. Animal cells do not have cell walls or chloroplasts.

- Plants are useful to humans for food and other non-food-related products. Plants are the basis of the food chain.

ASSESSMENT TASK AND RUBRIC: This seven-part paper/pencil task was used by a fifth-grade teacher to assess understanding of many of the concepts she taught in the unit. In Part I, students show their understanding of the structure and function of four plant parts. In Part II, they show their ability to classify leaves using a dichotomous key. In Part III, students describe what they know about tree rings, and in Parts IV and V, they describe some of the ways that plants are useful to society. Part VI asks students to compare the structure of plant cells with animal cells using a graphic organizer, and in Part VII, students tell how microscopes were used to enhance learning.

The task assessed content understanding and application; similarities and differences between living things; process and thinking skills; use of technology; the relationship between science, technology, and society; the nature of science; and change over time.

The rubric identifies indicators of learning for each of the seven parts of the task and was designed to enable students to self-assess and compare their scores with the scores and comments provided by the teacher. Following the assessment task, students were divided into groups based on which parts of the task they did not understand and were given opportunities for relearning. Students who had a perfect score on the task were given opportunities for extended learning through activities of their choice.

What I Know About Plants

Part I: Draw a flowering plant. Include and label four important parts.

Tell the function of each part:

a. stem

b. leaves

c. roots

d. flowers

Part II: Classify the leaves shown in the drawings below. Identify one property you will use to sort the leaves into two categories. Write the name of the property and put the letter of each leaf into the boxes that show whether the leaves have or do not have the property.

Note to teacher: Add drawings of leaves A and B parallel venation, C, D, and E palmate venation.

Data Table for Classification

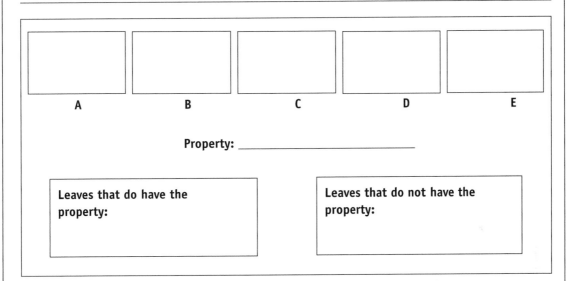

Property: _____

Leaves that do have the property:	Leaves that do not have the property:

Part III: How do tree rings indicate the age of a tree? How does a tree create rings?

Part IV: List three ways that plants are useful to humans (other than as food).

1.

2.

3.

Part V: List three common foods that are plants and tell what part of a plant each one is.

Data Table

Food	Plant Part
(1)	(1)
(2)	(2)
(3)	(3)

Part VI: Complete the Venn diagram. Identify at least two ways that plant and animal cells are structurally alike. List two ways they are structurally different. The figure below includes possible answers.

Comparing Plant and Animal Cells

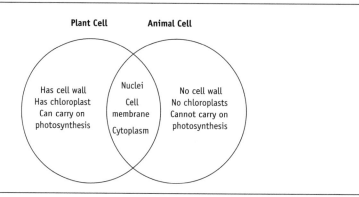

Part VII: Describe how using a microscope helps you to understand plants better.

Rubric for Plant Unit Assessment

The rubric developed for the performance task is an analytic scoring rubric. Each indicator of learning is given a score. (Note: Indicators of learning that are considered to be more important can be weighted, such as X 2.)

The student:

Part I:
- Drew a plant showing leaves, stem, roots, and flowers   1   0
- Labeled each of the four parts correctly   4   3   2   1   0
- Wrote the function of each part   4   3   2   1   0

Part II:
- Identified a property   1   0
- Classified each of the five leaves into 2 categories   2   1   0

Part III:
- Explained tree rings   2   1   0

Part IV:
- Listed three ways plants are useful   3   2   1   0

Part V:
- Listed three common foods and their parts   3   2   1   0

Part VI:
- Listed two ways plant and animal cells are alike   2   1   0
- Listed two ways plant and animal cells are different   2   1   0
- Described function of a microscope   1   0

Total Point Value: 25

PERFORMANCE ASSESSMENT #2—
CREATE A CREATURE—
UNDERSTANDING ADAPTATION

DESCRIPTION AND PURPOSE: The performance task, Create a Creature—Understanding Adaptation, follows a study of the solar system and includes a research component that identifies the unique characteristics of the planets. The task assumes that students have prior knowledge of the concept of adaptation from life science, since it requires them to apply the concept in the context of Earth science in a creative way.

The purpose of the task is to assess the student's ability to apply the concept of adaptation to the creation of a creature that can survive on one of the planets besides Earth. The task requires students to consider the unique features of one of the planets and to design adaptations that an alien would need to survive on the planet.

PROCEDURES: The task has two parts. In Part I, students should work in small groups to research the features of each of the planets and Pluto (optional). As a class, they should complete a chart similar to the one in Figure 6.5 that shows the density, surface temperature, gravity, cloud cover, length of year, and length of day for each planet along with other features that are unique to each planet.

In Part II, students create a creature that is adapted to conditions on any planet other than Earth. Students are asked to consider at least five features from the planet information chart and create a creature with features that make it possible for it to survive there. This task may be done in small groups, with partners, or individually.

PRODUCT: Students will create a detailed drawing of their creature, give it a name, and be prepared to show and describe five adaptations related to the conditions on the planet the creature calls home. When describing their creature, students should identify each adaptation and tell how it enables the creature to survive on the planet they have selected. For example, a creature may have adapted to a planet with extremely cold temperatures by having a very thick coat of fur or other natural or synthetic covering (adaptation) to keep it from freezing (how it aids survival).

MATERIALS: Planet Information Chart; poster or chart paper; pencils; crayons or markers.

PRESENTING THE TASK: Teachers should be sure that students understand the importance of creating creatures with features that relate to the characteristics of the planets found on the information chart shown in Figure 6.5. It is important for students to be able to explain each feature as an adaptation that enables the creature to

(Continued)

(Continued)

survive, since this is how they will show their understanding of the concept.

ASSESSING THE PERFORMANCE: The task includes an instructional component through which skills of media literacy can be assessed, such as the ability to access and use information from a variety of sources and the ability to use a variety of media tools to create messages effectively. Indicators of learning related to science that can be assessed through the completion and presentation of the project include an understanding of the concept of adaptation, skills of technological design, and communication skills.

Figure 6.5   Planet Information Chart

Planet	Density g/cm³ (Earth = 5.52g/cm³)	Surface Temp (max/min) Degrees K	Gravity (Earth=1)	Atmospheric Components	Cloud Cover	Length of Year (Earth Days)	Length of Day (Earth Days)	Other Features
Mercury								
Venus								
Mars								
Jupiter								
Saturn								
Uranus								
Neptune								
Pluto (optional)								
Earth								

PERFORMANCE ASSESSMENT ■
AS BENCHMARK ASSESSMENT

Performance assessments may be used as benchmark assessments. This type of assessment consists of a task or series of tasks administered to a group of students within a school or school system in order to determine the level of mastery of important concepts or skills by a specified grade level.

School district administrators with the aid of classroom teachers and parents often identify important learning goals they want students in their schools to master. These goals are not unlike national and state standards, but they are specifically identified by school and community stakeholders who consider them to be of greatest importance for student success. Benchmark assessments enable administrators and teachers to monitor learning at pivotal points as well as to assess the effectiveness of the curriculum and classroom instruction.

CHARACTERISTICS OF ■
BENCHMARK ASSESSMENTS

Benchmark assessments are thoughtfully developed tasks or activities that address specific goals in a student-friendly context. They are often presented as class projects or problem-based investigations that engage students in a stimulating and stress-free environment that enables them to develop or reinforce concepts and skills that are not being assessed while demonstrating an understanding of concepts and skills that are being assessed.

A few of the characteristics of worthwhile benchmark assessments are described here.

- Credible: Do the tasks measure what they say they measure? Are the scoring criteria and rubrics clear, descriptive, and related to important goals and standards? Does the scoring system allow for reliable discrimination of degrees of quality?
- Context: Do the tasks simulate authentic challenges faced by professionals, consumers, or citizens?
- Feasible: Are directions clear, concise, and meaningful to students?
- Performance-Based: Do the tasks focus on students' abilities to produce quality products or performances?
- Useful: Do rubrics enable students to a self-assess? Is feedback provided that identifies strengths and weaknesses for self-improvement?
- Valid: Do tasks address the important concepts and skills taught through instruction? Do the tasks provide sufficient evidence of student ability and levels of mastery?
- Verify Learning: Do the assessment tasks challenge students and enable them to display or demonstrate learning of content and skills? Do the assessments enable students to show understanding and application of learning?

■ SAMPLE BENCHMARK ASSESSMENT

The example shows a benchmark assessment that was designed to assess learning of second-grade students throughout a school district. This multidimensional assessment task is composed of a series of activities that engage students in investigating their personal behaviors and suggesting ways to solve a problem.

Overview and Goals

In this performance task, students are invited by the school district superintendent to investigate the use of paper in their class and suggest ways to reduce, reuse, or recycle paper in their classroom, school, and other schools throughout the district. This performance task was designed by teachers to assess three important district goals:

- Access and Use Information Effectively
- Think Critically
- Communicate Effectively

Science Standards-Related Concepts and Applications of Learning

Besides assessing the primary goals, the assessment addresses and builds a deeper understanding of a number of concepts and skills found in national and state science standards including

- change, constancy, and measurement
- the relationship between science and technology
- science as a human endeavor
- the ability to apply methods of scientific inquiry and technological design to investigate questions, solve problems, and analyze claims

Language arts goals specifically addressed through the activities are writing to communicate for a variety of purposes and using reading, writing, speaking, and listening skills to research and apply information for specific purposes.

Rubrics for the Performance Assessment

There are two rubrics for the performance assessment. The rubric in Figure 6.6 identifies the indicators of learning for the three goals that are being assessed. In this case, the indicators of learning are scored using a one-zero analytic scoring system. If the indicator is acceptable, it is scored with a one; if it is not shown or unacceptable, it receives a zero. Note that some of the indicators of learning were considered by teachers to be of more importance than others. These are weighted or assigned a higher score than other indicators.

The second rubric shown in Figure 6.7 is a student self-assessment. This rubric is given to students to guide them through the five assignments included in the task. The tool provides a way for them to document and assess their work.

BENCHMARK ASSESSMENT: I CAN MAKE A DIFFERENCE

DESCRIPTION OF THE PERFORMANCE

In response to a memo from the superintendent, students will collect and sort discarded materials in their classroom for a week to gain a better understanding of how much waste is generated by a class of students in a week. Students will interview adults or older students to learn more about reducing, reusing, and recycling. They will create a poster identifying a related problem and suggest ways to solve the problem. They will write a letter to the superintendent to communicate their ideas regarding ways to reduce, reuse, and/or recycle in their own classroom and school.

TEACHER DIRECTIONS

Standards-related content provides a context for this performance task. Teachers may want to assess knowledge or skills inherent in these goals and standards, but they are not directly assessed through the performance. The district outcomes are the focus of this assessment.

Student data sheets should be designed by teachers or by teachers and students for each of the activities. The information on the rubric will guide in their development. Teachers should become familiar with the assessment task and the Rubric for District Outcomes. During the course of the activities, the teacher should complete a scoring sheet for each student. Each student should complete the Self-Assessment.

Time

One class period for approximately eight school days. The task begins with pre-collecting activities that will take from two to three days (Wednesday–Friday). Then collecting and analyzing should be done the following Monday–Friday.

Materials

Chart paper or poster for a class KWL chart (what I know; what I want to know; what I learned) ; letter writing paper; spring scales or balances and mass sets; teacher- or student-supplied glue, markers, scissors, crayons, and pencils

For each student: a student notebook with recording and data sheets that correspond with the assignments on the rubric; one sheet of 24 x 28–inch poster board; gallon-size zip top bag; plastic grocery bag; self-adhesive hook

(Continued)

(Continued)

RATIONALE FOR PERFORMANCE TASK
All matter on the Earth is connected. Students need to understand that there is no "away" and that they can make a difference in the amount of waste and garbage they make by reducing, reusing, and recycling. Providing opportunities for students to raise and answer questions relative to waste reduction is imperative. Students need to seek answers by accessing information, making careful observations, collecting and analyzing data, drawing conclusions, and making decisions based on the conclusions. Making decisions involves choices, and choices have consequences, some of which are more serious than others. Students should be able to communicate their ideas.

PRIOR EXPERIENCE
This performance assumes that students have had experiences with:

- notebook writing to record ideas and data
- creating action plans
- interviewing
- the three R's (reduce, reuse, recycle)
- letter writing
- experience with units of instruction in Grade 1
- exposure to district curriculum: Matter Matters—Grade 2
- visit to recycling center

Presenting the Performance Tasks

Activity One

1. Read a memo from the Superintendent to the class. Facilitate the K portion of KWL: "What Do You Know About Garbage/Trash" (3 R's, Landfills, and so forth).

2. Record student questions on the W section of the chart as they arise throughout the week.

3. Post the KWL chart in the classroom for ongoing reference; update and correct as needed.

Sample Memo From Superintendent

TO: Second-Grade Class
FROM: The District Superintendent
Re: Garbage Problem

Students, it has come to my attention that the students in our schools are generating a large amount of garbage. The PTA and I want to try to solve this problem. We are requesting your help.

We want you to collect your garbage for one week, study the results, and make suggestions of how students can reduce, reuse, or recycle as much of the garbage as possible. Your suggestions will be passed along to other students in the district.

Please respond by _____. Include a statement of the problem you investigated, something you learned through your investigations, and a plan with one or more suggestions for reducing, reusing, and/or recycling garbage in your school.

Thank you so much. We appreciate your help with this problem.

Activity Two

1. Have students clean desks to get rid of garbage and trash the day before collecting is to begin.

2. Use a self-adhesive plastic hook on each student's desk to hang one plastic grocery bag for non-wet trash collection. Provide one zip top bag per person for wet garbage (snacks, etc.).

3. Provide a separate "biohazard" container in the room for tissues, bandages, paper towels, and so forth.

4. Discuss the meanings for the words "garbage" and "trash."

    garbage, n: a. food wastes, as from a kitchen; b. refuse; trash

    trash, n: a. worthless or discarded material or objects; refuse or rubbish; b. something broken off or removed to be discarded, especially plant trimmings (American Heritage Dictionary)

    Operational Definition: For our purposes, "garbage" will mean any discarded material (food, waste, and trash).

5. Students should complete the first thinking page in class. (What do the words *reduce*, *reuse*, and *recycle* mean to you?)

6. Students should complete the homework page over the weekend. Ask students to interview someone in their family to find out in what way(s) the family disposes of garbage (all discarded materials).

7. Tell students they will receive points for completing the assignment and for answering the question. Review the first assignment shown on the Student Rubric.

(Continued)

(Continued)

Activity Three

1. On Monday morning, remove garbage cans and recycling bins from classroom. Students will begin to save their own garbage in the appropriate bags.

2. Review the terms *reduce, reuse,* and *recycle*. Using information students gathered from their interviews, operationally define each term and discuss some ways that families reduce, reuse, and recycle. For example:

   - reduce: to diminish in size, amount, extent, or number
   - reuse: to use again especially after reclaiming or reprocessing
   - recycle: to pass again through a series of changes or treatments as to process in order to gain material for human use; to recover; to adapt to a new use

3. Collect homework page.

Activity Four

1. On Monday or Tuesday, children should choose one question from the W portion of the class KWL chart to write on the Interview Sheet (Who I interviewed; What I learned). The students will use this page to record their interviews of one or more adults or older students outside the classroom. They may wish to generate a list of people they might interview. For example, they may interview a family member, a neighbor, a teacher, or a friend's parent. Students may take notes or tape record interviews.

2. Review the second assignment on the Student Rubric. The next day, students should be able to tell who they interviewed and tell what the person or persons said about their question.

Activity Five

1. On Wednesday, students will weigh their total garbage and record the date and the mass in grams on the Garbage Record Sheet data table (Day; Mass of Garbage).

2. Introduce the poster assignment. Review the Student Rubric for the poster assignment.

3. Tell students to design a poster that (a) states a problem relating to creating too much garbage, (b) shows a possible solution on the same poster, and (c) uses both words and pictures(s).

Have them make a rough draft in pencil, then make corrections in spelling. After the draft has been checked by the teacher, students should put the final copy on the poster board using markers or crayons. The poster should be neat.

Activity Six

1. On Thursday, have students draw, on the Reuse and Recycle Sheet, three things that can be reused or recycled and tell how each thing can be reused or recycled. Show students Rubric #4 for listing three things and telling how each can be reused or recycled.

2. Continue to work on poster.

Activity Seven

1. On Friday, students weigh their own total garbage and record their data on the Garbage Record Sheet data table. Make a bar graph for data for Wednesday and Friday (before sorting).

2. Students should sort their garbage according to the places in which each item could be disposed (following classroom recycling plan). Students should tell how they sorted.

3. As a class, determine "official" sorting categories according to the school's recycling plan. Return recycling bins to classroom and have students place recyclables and reusable materials in the appropriate places.

4. Each student should place all remaining garbage back in his or her own bag and weigh it. The weight should be recorded on the data table on the Garbage Record Sheet. Complete the last column of the graph.

5. Bring back garbage cans. All students dispose of remaining garbage in cans.

6. As a class, add total weight of garbage in the classroom before the sort and after the sort. Compare the totals and then subtract the "after sort" total from the "before sort" total. The difference between the two totals gives you the amount of garbage that has been recycled or reused.

   Stress the difference students CAN make by recycling and reusing items. Multiply results by the number of classrooms in your school for a rough estimate of the garbage generated by one school in a week.

(Continued)

Activity Eight

1. Refer to the original memo from the superintendent and remind students that the superintendent expects a written response based on their new insights.

2. Show students Rubric #5 and describe the expectations for the letter they will write: identify the problem, write what you learned, and suggest a way or ways to solve the problem.

3. Student should write a rough draft of their letters and then edit the letter using the Editing Checklist.

4. Students should copy their letters in final form using appropriate capital letters, correct punctuation, and correct spelling.

QUESTIONS FOR REFLECTION, APPLICATION, AND MEANING

1. Based on what you learned from your investigation, predict how much garbage and trash are generated in one week by all the students in our school.

2. What are some ways to reduce the amount of garbage we create in our classroom and in our homes?

3. What types of things can be reused or recycled in our classrooms and in our homes?

4. What can you do to help solve the garbage problem?

5. Why would someone decide not to recycle?

6. What happens to the paper, glass, and aluminum we recycle?

7. How is our community affected when people don't recycle?

8. How can you inform others about the importance of reducing, reusing, and recycling garbage and trash?

SOURCE: Reprinted with permission of the Curriculum Writers/Community Unit School District 303, St. Charles, IL.

Figure 6.6	Rubric for District Outcomes: I Can Make a Difference				
Instructional Goals and Indicators of Learning		1	0	Weight	Score
Access and Use Information Effectively **The student**:					
Showed evidence of interview (notes, tape, etc.)					
Recorded data on data table (weights of garbage)					
Graphed data from data table correctly				x 3	
Think Critically **The student:**					
Wrote a question from KWL chart for interview					
Drew three things on Reused/Recycle Sheet				x 3	
Told how each can be reused or recycled				x 3	
Sorted garbage on day five appropriately					
Communicate Effectively **The student:**					
Told what he or she learned from interview on the Question and Interview Sheet					
Designed a poster that: states a problem shows an answer includes words and pictures					
Wrote a letter that: identifies the problem tells what he or she learned suggests ways to solve the problem uses capital letters appropriately uses punctuation correctly uses correct spelling				x 2 x 2	
Possible Score: 25 Total Score:					

Figure 6.7   Self-Assessment: Student Rubric for I Can Make A Difference

Assignments	Completed Task	Not Completed	Comments
#1 Homework Page			
I completed and returned my family interview			
I wrote what I learned			
#2 Question and Interview			
I wrote a question I wondered about			
I interviewed an older student or adult			
I told the class what I learned			
#3 Poster Assignment			
My poster states a problem			
My poster shows an answer to the problem			
My poster is neat			
My poster has both words and pictures			
#4 Thinking About Problems and Solutions			
I drew three things that can be reused or recycled			
I told how each of the three things can be reused or recycled		.	
#5 Letter to the Superintendent			
I identified the problem			
I told what I learned			
I included one or more solutions			
My final letter has capital letters			
My final letter has correct punctuation			
My final letter has correct spelling			

7

Planning and Implementing Formative Assessment

An important factor in educational reform is teacher awareness and understanding of formative assessment as a powerful tool for enhancing learning. Formative assessment can be used effectively to raise standards when teachers are proficient in using a variety of assessment strategies and have a system for managing the progress of each student.

In a goal-centered, cooperative environment where teachers and students work together toward the mastery of goals and standards, students are able to take responsibility for their learning and reach higher levels of achievement. Formative assessment tools and strategies provide teachers with data and information needed to provide feedback to students, monitor learning, and modify instruction to meet the needs and interests of a diverse population of students.

CHARACTERISTICS OF HIGH-QUALITY INSTRUCTION AND ASSESSMENT ■

As with instructional units and lessons, assessments must be thoughtfully planned. Both unit and lesson models for planning instruction have sections for identifying and describing the types of goal- or standards-related assessments that will be used to gather information about student learning and the effectiveness of instruction. The new vision for assessment describes formative assessment as a tool for enhancing learning and, as such, should be a critical component of instructional planning.

Hammerman (2006a) identified eight research-based steps to the design and development of high-quality teaching and learning, which include the development of an assessment system. An abbreviated list of the steps in the achievement model is shown here.

- Address clear and appropriate learning goals
- Build concepts and principles
- Develop process and thinking skills and practice dispositions valued by the scientific community
- Accommodate diversity through meaningful contexts
- Use a variety of methods and strategies that engage and challenge students intellectually
- Develop thinking and problem-solving skills through questioning; make sense of learning
- Design an assessment system to provide feedback to students to monitor and guide learning and to assess the effectiveness of instruction
- Use equipment and resources in a safe and stress-free environment to enhance teaching and learning

The first three steps require one to have a good understanding of standards-based concepts and principles as well as strategies for developing important process and thinking skills and valued disposition. Once clear targets are established, the developer should give thought to summative measures of student learning. Consider: In what ways will students show that they have mastered the instructional goals?

As learning activities and experiences are selected or developed to address key concepts and skills, careful consideration should be given to the formative assessments that will be embedded throughout instruction to provide information about student learning and the effectiveness of instruction. The formative assessments should provide multiple and varied ways for students to show what they know and are able to do.

The following questions may be useful in guiding the selection of formative assessment strategies:

- In what ways can students demonstrate concept understanding, skill improvement or mastery, desirable habits of mind, and connections between science and their personal lives, technology, and the global community?
- What tools and strategies can be used to capture evidence of student thinking and learning?

PLANNING FORMATIVE ASSESSMENT ■

Review of Assessment Strategies

Figure 7.1 provides a review of formative assessment strategies that briefly describes the types of evidence of learning that can be collected through each type of assessment and a few examples in the context of K–8 science. The chart provides a reference for selecting formative assessment strategies that will provide evidence of learning of important goals and standards throughout instruction.

Figure 7.1 Tools and Strategies for Formative Assessment		
Type of Assessment	*Type of Evidence Captured*	*Examples in K–8 Science*
Observation Checklist	• Dispositions and behaviors • Completion of tasks	• Ability to work well in a cooperative learning group • Respect for living things and equipment • Willingness to share ideas and assist others • Teacher or student check of work
Interviews, Dialogue, and Informal Questioning	• Understanding of directions and procedures • Accuracy of explanations or data • Concept understanding • Appropriate use of skills • Accuracy of applications and connections	• Informal dialogue during investigations • Asking questions for clarification of process, data, or meaning • Small group or individualized teacher-student or student-student discussion • Peer review or pair/share
Science Notebooks and Lab Reports	• Understanding of concepts and skills through written work, drawings, and graphics • Ability to generate and investigate inquiry questions • Mastery levels of contextual and problem-solving skills • Literacy and critical thinking skills • Creative thinking	• Notebook entries related to investigations, experiences, and research • Logical and reasonable explanations of processes, data, and conclusions • Rational and creative thinking in discussions of applications and connections

(Continued)

Figure 7.1   (Continued)

Type of Assessment	Type of Evidence Captured	Examples in K–8 Science
Products, Projects, and Presentations	• Ability to access and use new information purposefully • Ability to design and develop products that show understanding and application of concepts • Creativity and problem-solving skills • Ability to apply learning to new situations • Organizational and verbal skills • Ability to use technology	• Student-created brochures, posters, models, investigations, and reports • New inventions for solving problems • Use of technology and technological design • Science fair projects • Research and extended learning based on new questions • Demonstrations of concept understanding and skills
Performance Tasks	• Ability to apply learning to new problems • Concept understanding • Meaningful application of concepts • Ability to apply contextual and thinking skills • Reasoning and problem solving	• Investigations that develop and apply concepts and skills • Investigations of problems or issues • Written explanations and graphic representations that show understanding of concepts or relationships between concepts
Criterion-Referenced Tests and Writing Prompts	• Understanding of concepts and relationships between concepts • Plausible solutions to problems • Applications and meaning of concepts	• Accuracy of responses to test items • Responses to questions or prompts that show thought and understanding • Drawings, graphics, and explanations of process, data, graphs, meaning, and applications

A PLANNING GUIDE ■
FOR FORMATIVE ASSESSMENT

Units of instruction address learning goals and standards that are statements of what students should know and be able to do. Throughout instruction, essential questions and indicators of learning related to the goals and standards can be assessed to understand what and how students are learning. Formative assessments provide feedback to students about their learning and abundant information on which to make decisions.

Figure 7.2 offers a planning guide for including formative assessment tools and strategies in a unit of instruction. The first column provides a space to record the essential questions or indicators of learning around which the unit will be developed. The second column identifies the type of assessment tools or strategies that will be used, and the third column describes the evidence of learning that will be collected.

Figure 7.2   A Planning Guide for Formative Assessment

Essential Questions or Indicators of Learning	Type of Assessment	Evidence of Learning

■ A PLANNING GUIDE FOR A UNIT ON CELLS

Figure 7.3 shows a completed planning guide for a unit on cells. Standards-related concepts that provide a focus for instruction and assessment are identified. Indicators of learning based on important concepts and skills guide the instructional designer in the selection of investigations and experiences and the tools and strategies for formative assessment tools that will be embedded throughout instruction.

CONCEPTS FOR A MIDDLE SCHOOL UNIT ON CELLS

- Some living things consist of a single cell and need food, water, and air, a way to dispose of waste, and an environment in which they can live

- Microscopes make it possible to see that living things are made of cells

- Animals and plants have a great variety of body parts and internal structures that contribute to their being able to make food and reproduce

- All organisms are made of cells, the fundamental unit of life

- Most organisms are single cells, and other organisms, including humans, are multicellular

- Cells carry on the many functions needed to sustain life

- Cells grow and divide, making more cells

■ USING ASSESSMENT DATA TO MODIFY INSTRUCTION

Formative assessment tools and strategies are diagnostic tools since they provide a wealth of information about specific strengths and weaknesses. Feedback from formative assessments provides information from which decisions can be made. When data show that indicators of learning are not being met, there is a need to modify instruction. Data may also show that some students are not being challenged. In either case, instruction should be modified for large groups, small groups, or individuals.

Formative assessments inform instruction and point to the need to differentiate instruction. Any adjustments in instruction should relate directly to the goals and objectives of the unit of study. Students may suggest learning activities or experiences that are of interest to them for relearning or extended learning, or teachers may offer choices of activities that address specific the needs of the learner.

A few instructional strategies that can be used to accommodate students who need to strengthen concept understanding or skills are shown here. Some of the approaches may be used to extend learning for students who need additional challenges.

Figure 7.3 Assessment Plan for a Unit on Cells		
Indicators of Student Learning	*Type of Assessment*	*Evidence of Learning*
Handles equipment carefully and uses equipment effectively	Checklist	Recording of careful handling and effective use of microscopes
Works well in cooperative group; makes contributions	Checklist	Recording of student behaviors and contributions in groups
Describes the characteristics of living things	Writing Prompt	Students distinguish between living and nonliving things and explain characteristics of living things
Knows the structure and function of cells and recognizes that cells are the building blocks of organisms	Performance Task	Students observe a variety of plant and animal cells under a microscope Students draw and label parts of a cell, research and describe functions of cell parts, and explain how cells function in single- and multi-celled organisms
Knows the differences between plant and animal cells	Graphic Organizer	Students draw or use a graphic organizer to compare structures of plant and animal cells
Keeps careful, detailed records of procedures and learning	Notebook Entries	Students record questions, describe investigations, collect and show data, and explain conclusions Students apply learning, make connections, and explain meaning
Makes a model of a cell and describes the structure and function of cells and cell organelles	Product and Presentation	Students make models of cells, including the organelles, using a variety of materials; the product is accurate and includes appropriate labels Students describe the structure and function of cell(s) and the organelles shown in their model Students answer questions related to structure and function of cells
Demonstrates analogical thought	Performance Task	Students use a graphic organizer to show how a cell is like X (a large system) Students show and describe how each part of the cell functions like a component of the system

■ PROJECT CHOICES

There may be more than one way for students to address a specific learning goal. Project choices provide options for learning that may be of greater of interest to students than a standard approach for all. When students are offered choices, they are more likely to take ownership for learning.

For example, during the unit on cells, students may be offered a variety of ways to address the indicator of learning: *The students will make a model of a cell and describe the structure and function of cells and cell organelles.* Six alternatives that address the indicator of learning and appeal to a variety of learning styles and multiple intelligences are described.

1. **Whole Cell Catalog:** Create a catalog for something for which there may not yet be a market such as the major organelles in a cell. Create catalog pages to sell two of the major organelles.

2. **Edible Cell:** Construct a cell model using edible materials to represent the cell and its major organelles. For example: a cake with different types of candies to represent each organelle.

3. **Journey Into the Cell:** Write and illustrate a creative story similar to *The Magic School Bus* series where people and animals are miniaturized and travel inside and around cells.

4. **Infomercial About the Cell**: Script, direct, tape, and edit a commercial to advertise cell organelles. Include information about their structure and function.

5. **PowerPoint on the Cell:** Create a PowerPoint presentation that summarizes what you learned about the structure and function of the major organelles of a cell.

6. **Cell Poster:** Design and create giant poster showing the major organelles of the cell. Display your work

■ ADJUSTING ASSIGNMENTS

Information gained from formative assessments may lead to adjustable assignments. Assignments can be modified to strengthen weak areas or to challenge students beyond the basic instruction. Adjusted assignments should focus on basic concepts and skills that need to be developed or enhanced.

The chances of success for each learner are increased when work is challenging and success is within reach. Adjusting assignments to meet the needs of struggling students decreases the chances of "downshifting" and the sense of helplessness that they often feel when a challenge is beyond their capabilities.

STATIONS FOR ACTIVE LEARNING ■

Stations are places around the classroom where a sequence of topic-related activities or visuals are set up. Generally, each has a set of materials and directions for the task that is to be accomplished. Each task should have a worthwhile purpose related to the development or application of a concept, development of skills, or both. For example, each station may have a microscope with a prepared slide that shows a single phase of mitosis. Students would need to visit all stations to record the complete process.

Tasks should require students to manipulate materials and use tools of technology, make and record observations, collect data or use numbers, make drawings or models, apply concepts, and summarize learning.

DIFFERENTIATING ■
INSTRUCTION THROUGH CENTERS

Centers are places where the work can be designed to fit the learner's needs. Centers provide opportunities for students to:

- remediate, enhance, or extend knowledge of concepts
- explore connections, applications, and careers
- pursue interests and explore new ways of knowing
- practice skills and dispositions
- be challenged at their ability level
- solve problems and invent new products or strategies
- make choices and work at their own pace
- manipulate different types of materials
- apply complex thinking processes

Centers may be set up for relearning important concepts and skills, enhancing understanding, or extending learning. They may provide materials and resources for students to design and conduct experiments to answer their questions. Some of the different types of centers that can be designed for science are:

- Topics or theme centers with hands-on activities to develop or deepen concept understanding
- Computer-based learning centers with multimedia resources for remediation or extended learning
- Resource centers with reading materials at a variety of levels
- Art media table to create artifacts such as models, technological designs, or new inventions
- Skill centers for practice of important contextual learning skills
- Project centers with writing and drawing tools and various types and sizes of paper for creating newspapers, brochures, booklets, posters, letters, articles, or poems
- Listening centers with music or readings from both fictional and factual content
- Free choice centers with materials and equipment for experimenting, discovering, and inventing

Observation checklists, data sheets, or notebook entries, demonstrations of knowledge or ability, and formal and nonformal discussion can be used to assess work at stations. Students should assess their progress in meeting instructional goals.

■ CREATING CONTRACTS

Another option for modifying instruction based on feedback is for teachers and students to work together to design contracts for learning to address specific needs. Contracts provide students with clear goals and expectations for learning, choices for approaches to learning, ownership of their learning, and responsibility for managing time and tasks. Individually designed contracts identify:

- clear learning goals
- a list of concepts to be learned and skills to be developed
- an action plan
- a timeline for completing the tasks
- the resources and materials the student will need to accomplish the tasks
- how learning will be assessed

■ FORMATIVE ASSESSMENT AND ACCOUNTABILITY

When assessments are embedded in instruction, students are often not aware that they are being assessed. To be useful, data must be collected for students individually, which means, whether they work alone, with a partner, or in small groups, each student should be personally responsible and accountable for completing tasks and recording information.

Five classroom situations related to instruction, assessment, and accountability are described.

Situation 1

For some investigations and activities, students will work alone and show their work along with detailed visual(s) and written descriptions to demonstrate concept understanding. In this case, students get the materials they need, perform the task, and record all information on data sheets or in a notebook. If assessment tasks are long term, as in the case of germinating seeds and recording observations and data over time, teachers might review data sheets or notebooks periodically with students to determine how students are progressing and to provide feedback.

Situation 2

If stations are used as part of instruction, students should visit each station for a specified amount of time on a rotating basis and record individual responses on data sheets or in notebooks. The limited time at each station might pose a problem for some students. They should be given a second opportunity to visit one or more stations, if necessary. Problems may occur if the materials at a station were altered or if something were missing prior to a student reaching the station. The monitoring of the stations by the teacher or assistant is an important consideration for this type of instruction.

Situation 3

Projects may be done individually or with a partner or group and presented to an audience of peers. Presentations should include a statement of purpose and the design of the project and evidence of learning. Each member of the group should contribute equally to the presentation. The presentation should include clear and accurate explanations, products, and visuals. They may include the use of technology, demonstrations, or audience participation. Students may be given a set of guidelines for the project or a rubric to clarify expectations use as a tool for self-assessment.

Situation 4

Some investigations or approaches to learning, such as problem-based learning, are best done with a partner or with a small group. In this case, students should work together to perform the tasks, but each student should be required to record data, make sense of group-collected data, and be prepared to describe the conclusions and applications of learning. Each student should complete response sheets, record all pertinent information in a notebook, or complete a lab report. A rubric may be designed to guide students and clarify expectations. The rubric can be used for self-assessment.

Situation 5

Some tasks may be done in a small cooperative group with the group, as a whole, required to agree on a response. In this case, the response generated by the group is the response for each student. If one or more members of the group do not agree with the group decision, the student or students should be allowed to submit individual response sheets showing their responses. This unique situation needs to be considered by teachers, since students become frustrated or discouraged when they are given a score based on responses with which they don't agree.

References and Further Reading

American Association for the Advancement of Science. (1990). *Project 2061: Science for all Americans*. New York: Oxford University Press.

American Association for the Advancement of Science. (1993). *Project 2061: Benchmarks for science literacy*. New York: Oxford University Press.

American Association for the Advancement of Science and National Science Teachers Association. (2001). *Project 2061: Atlas of science literacy*. Washington, DC: AAAS Press.

Anderson, O., & Stewart, J. (1997). A neurocognitive perspective on current learning theory and science instructional strategies. *Science Education, 81*(1), 67–90.

Anderson, R. D. (2002). Reforming science teaching: What research says about inquiry. *Journal of Science Teacher Education, 13*(1), 1–12.

Armstrong, T. (1998). *Awakening genius in the classroom*. Alexandria, VA: Association for Supervision and Curriculum Development.

Armstrong, T. (2003). The *multiple intelligences of reading and writing*. Alexandria, VA: Association for Supervision and Curriculum Development.

Audet, R. H., & Jordan, L. K. (2003). *Standards in the classroom: An implementation guide for teachers of science and mathematics*. Thousand Oaks, CA: Corwin Press.

Banilower, E. R., Boyd, S. E., Pasley, J. D., & Weiss, I. R. (Prepublication copy, 2006). *Lessons from a decade of mathematics and science reform: A capstone report. For the local systemic change through teacher enhancement initiative*. Chapel Hill, NC: Horizon Research, Inc.

Banks, J. A., Cookson, P., Gay, G., Hawley, W. D., Irvine, J. J., Neito, S., et al. (2001). Diversity within unity. *Phi Delta Kappan, 83*(3), 196–203.

Bellanca, J., & Fogarty, R. (2002). *Blueprints for achievement in the cooperative classroom*. Arlington Heights, IL: SkyLight Professional Development.

Birman, B. F., Desimone, L., Porter, A. D., & Garet, M. S. (2000). Designing professional development that works. *Educational Leadership, 58*(9), 28–32.

Black, P., Harrison, C., Lee, C., Marshall, B., & Wiliam, D. (2004). Working inside the black box. *Phi Delta Kappan, 85*(1), 9–21.

Black, P., & Wiliam, D. (1998). Inside the black box: Raising standards through classroom assessment. *Phi Delta Kappan, 80*(2), 139–148.

Blair, J. (2000). How teaching matters: Bringing the classroom back into discussion of teacher quality. *Education Week, 20*(8), 24.

Bloom, B. S. (Ed). (1956). *Taxonomy of educational objectives, handbook 1: Cognitive domain.* New York: David McKay Company, Inc.

Brophy, J. (1986). Teacher influences on student achievement. *American Psychologist, 41*(10), 1067–1077.

Burke, K. (2001). *Tips for managing your classroom.* Arlington Heights, IL: SkyLight Professional Development.

Burke, K. (2006). *From standards to rubrics in six steps.* Thousand Oaks, CA: Corwin Press.

Burns, M. (2005). Looking at how students reason. *Educational Leadership, 63*(3), 26–31.

Bybee, R. W. (2002). *Learning science and the science of learning.* Alexandria, VA: National Science Teachers Association Press.

Caine, R. N., & Caine, G. (1991). *Teaching and the human brain.* Alexandria, VA: Association for Supervision and Curriculum Development.

Caine, R. N., & Caine, G. (1997). *Education on the edge of possibility.* Alexandria, VA: Association for Supervision and Curriculum Development

Chappuis, J. (2005). Helping students understand assessment. *Educational Leadership, 63*(3), 39–43.

Chappuis, S., & Stiggins, R. (2005). Putting testing in perspective: It's for learning. *Principal Leadership, 6*(2), 15–20.

Committee on Education. (2004). *Lost in space: Science education in New York City public schools.* Report from the Council of the City of New York. Available from: http://www.nyccouncil.info/pdf_files/reports/lost%20 in%20space%20science%20report.pdf

Danielson, C. (2002). *Enhancing student achievement: A framework for school improvement.* Alexandria, VA: Association for Supervision and Curriculum Development.

Darling-Hammond, L. (1997). *The right to learn: A blueprint for creating schools that work.* San Francisco: Jossey-Bass.

Darling-Hammond, L., & McLaughlin, M. (1995). Policies that support professional development in an era of reform. *Phi Delta Kappan, 76*(8), 597–604.

DeHart Hurd, P. (1997). *Inventing science education for the new millennium.* New York: Teachers College Press.

Diamond, M., & Hopson, J. (1998). *Magic trees of the mind: How to nurture your child's intelligence, creativity, and healthy emotions from birth through adolescence.* New York: Dutton..

Enger, S., & Yager, R. E. (2001). *Assessing student understanding in science.* Thousand Oaks, CA: Corwin Press.

English, F. W. (1992). *Deciding what to teach and test.* Newbury Park, CA: Corwin Press.

Ermeling, B. A. (2005). *Transforming professional development for an American high school: A lesson study inspired, technology powered system for teacher learning.* Unpublished doctoral dissertation, University of California, Los Angeles

Gardner, H. (1993). *Multiple intelligences: The theory in practice.* New York: Basic Books.

Gardner, H. (1999). *Intelligence reframed: Multiple intelligences for the 21st century.* New York: Basic Books.

Gess-Newsome, J., & Lederman, N. (1999). *Examining pedagogical content knowledge.* Boston: Kluwer Academic Publishers

Goleman, D. (1995). *Emotional intelligence.* New York: Bantam Books.

Gregory, G., & Hammerman, E. (2008). *Differentiated instructional strategies in science.* Thousand Oaks, CA: Corwin Press.

Gutskey, T. R. (2000). *Evaluating professional development.* Thousand Oaks, CA: Corwin Press.

Hammerman, E. (2005). Linking classroom instruction and assessment to standardized testing. *Science Scope, 28*(4), 26–32.

Hammerman, E. (2006a). *Becoming a better science teacher.* Thousand Oaks, CA: Corwin Press.

Hammerman, E. (2006b). *Eight essentials of inquiry-based science.* Thousand Oaks, CA: Corwin Press.

Hammerman, E., & Musial, D. (2008). *Integrating science with mathematics and literacy: New visions for learning and assessment.* Thousand Oaks, CA: Corwin Press.

Herman, J. L., & Baker, E. L. (2005). Making benchmark testing work. *Educational Leadership, 63*(3), 48–54.

Holloway, J. (2000). How does the brain learn science? *Educational Leadership, 58*(3), 85–86.

Inspiration Software, Inc. (2003, July). *Graphic organizers: A review of scientifically based research.* Portland, OR: Author. Prepared by the Institute for the Advancement of Research in Education. Retrieved February 13, 2006, from http://www.inspriation.com

Jensen, E. (1989). *Teaching with the brain in mind.* Alexandria, VA: Association for Supervision and Curriculum Development.

Jensen, E. (2000). *Brain-based learning.* San Diego, CA: The Brain Store.

Joyce, B., & Showers, B. (1995). *Student achievement through staff development.* New York: Longman.

Klentschy, M., Garrison, L., & Maia Amaral, O. (2000). *Valle Imperial project in science (VIPS): Four-year comparison of student achievement data, 1995–1999.* El Centro, CA: El Centro School District.

Kohn, A. (1999). *Punished by rewards.* Boston: Houghton Mifflin.

Krueger, A., & Sutton, J., Eds. (2001). *Ed thoughts: What we know about science teaching and learning.* Aurora, CO: Mid-Continent Research for Education and Learning.

Lantz, H. B., Jr. (2004). *Rubrics for assessing student achievement in science grades K–12.* Thousand Oaks, CA: Corwin Press.

Lapp, D. (2001). Bridging the gaps. *Science Link, 12*(1), 1–3.

Lieberman, A. (1995). Practices that support teacher development. *Phi Delta Kappan, 76*(8), 591–696.

Loucks-Horsley, S., Hewson, P. W., Love, N., & Stiles, K. E. (1998). *Designing professional development for teachers of science and mathematics.* Thousand Oaks, CA: Corwin Press.

Madrazo, G. (1998). Embracing diversity. *The Science Teacher, 65*(3), 20–23.

Marzano, R. J. (2000). *Transforming classroom grading.* Alexandria, VA: Association for Supervision and Curriculum Development.

Marzano, R. J., & Kendall, J. S. (2007). *The new taxonomy of educational objectives.* Thousand Oaks, CA: Corwin Press.

Marzano, R. J., Pickering, D. J., & Pollock, J. E. (2001). *Classroom instruction that works.* Alexandria, VA: Association for Supervision and Curriculum Development.

McCormack, A. (1981). *Inventor's workshop.* Carthage, IL: Fearon Teacher Aids.

McTighe, J., & O'Connor, K. (2005). Seven practices for effective learning. *Educational Leadership, 63*(3), 10–17.

Musial, D., & Hammerman, E. (1992). Framing knowledge through moments: A model for teaching thinking in science. *Teaching Thinking and Problem Solving, 14*(2), 12–15.

Musial, D., & Hammerman, E. (1997). *Framing ways of knowing in problem-based learning.* Unpublished manuscript.

National Commission on Mathematics and Science Teaching for the 21st Century. (2000). *Before it's too late.* Washington, DC: Author.

National Research Council. (1996). *National science education standards.* Washington, DC: National Academy Press.

National Research Council. (2000). *How people learn.* Washington, DC: National Academies Press.

National Research Council. (2005). *How students learn science in the classroom.* Washington, DC: National Academies Press.

National Science Resources Center. (1997). *Science for all children.* Washington, DC: National Academy Press.

Parry, T., & Gregory, G. (1998). *Designing brain compatible learning.* Arlington Heights, IL: SkyLight Professional Development.

Reeves, D. B. (2006). Leading to change: Preventing 1,000 failures. *Educational Leadership, 64*(3), 88–89.

Reeves, D. B. (2008). Effective grading. *Educational Leadership, 65*(5), 85–87.

Rutherford, F. J., & Algren, A. (1990). *Science for all Americans.* New York: Oxford University Press.

Shulman, L. S. (1986). Those who understand: Knowledge growth in teaching. *Educational Researcher, 15*(2), 4–14.

Sparks, D., & Hirsh, S. (1997). *A new vision for staff development.* Alexandria, VA: Association for Supervision and Curriculum Development.

Stiggins, R., & Chappuis, J. (2006). What a difference a word makes. *National Staff Development Council, 27*(1), 10–11.

Stiggins, R. J. (1994). *Student-centered classroom assessment.* Upper Saddle River, NJ: Prentice-Hall, Inc.

Stiggins, R. J. (2002). Assessment crisis: The absence of assessment FOR learning. *Phi Delta Kappan, 83*(10), 758–765.

Stiggins, R. J. (2005). From formative assessment to assessment for learning: A path to success in standards-based schools. *Phi Delta Kappan, 87*(4), 324–328.

Stiggins, R. J. (2007). Five assessment myths and their consequences. *Education Week, 27*(8), 28–29.

Stronge, J. H. (2002). *Qualities of effective teachers.* Alexandria, VA: Association for Supervision and Curriculum Development.

Sylwester, R. (1995). *A celebration of neurons.* Alexandria, VA: Association for Supervision and Curriculum Development.

Sylwester, R. (2000). *A biological brain in a cultural classroom.* Thousand Oaks, CA: Corwin Press.

Tomlinson, C. (1999). *The differentiated classroom.* Alexandria, VA: Association for Supervision and Curriculum Development.

Torp, L. & Sage, S. (1998). *Problems as possibilities.* Alexandria, VA: Association for Supervision and Curriculum Development.

Weiss, I. R., Banilower, E. R., McMahon, K. C., & Smith, P. S. (2001). *Report of the 2000 national survey of science and mathematics education.* Chapel Hill, NC: Horizon Research, Inc.

Weiss, I. R., Pasley, J. D., Smith, P. S., Banilower, E. R., & Heck, D. J. (2003). *Looking inside the classroom: A study of K–12 mathematics and science education in the United States.* Chapel Hill, NC: Horizon Research, Inc.

Wenglinsky, H. (2000). *How teaching matters: Bringing the classroom back into discussion of teacher quality. A policy information center report.* Princeton, NJ: Educational Testing Service

Wiggins, G. (1992). Creating test worth taking. *Educational Leadership, 49*(8), 26–28.

Wolfe, P. (2001). *Brain matters.* Alexandria, VA: Association for Supervision and Curriculum Development.

Index

CORWIN
PRESS

The Corwin Press logo—a raven striding across an open book—represents the union of courage and learning. Corwin Press is committed to improving education for all learners by publishing books and other professional development resources for those serving the field of PreK–12 education. By providing practical, hands-on materials, Corwin Press continues to carry out the promise of its motto: **"Helping Educators Do Their Work Better."**